AF479308

New

York

Serenade

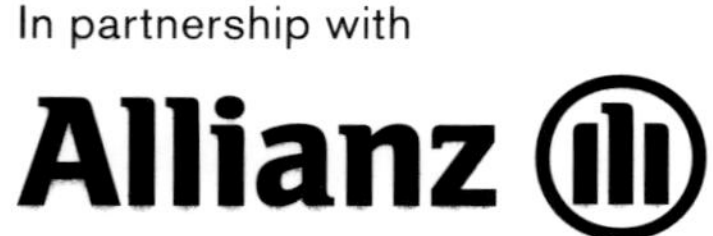
In partnership with
Allianz

New York Serenade

Ciro Frank Schiappa
Photographs

Michele Primi
Texts

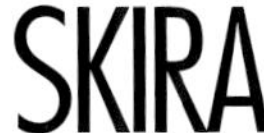

To Anita

Birthplaces   **Joel Meyerowitz**

Every age has its creative bursts of energy. In the 20th century we had—just
to name a few—the rise of cubism in Paris, German expressionism in Berlin,
and the Jazz Age in Chicago, New York, New Orleans, and the south. The Blues
ran through the south and made its way north. Abstract expressionism appeared
in New York, followed by pop art, minimalism, rock, and on and on, with every
generation discovering for itself the form that best defines it.
Often these new waves of expression are born far from the so-called hip city
centers. Then, as we have seen so many times, development, gentrification,
and rising prices push the artists out of these small neighborhoods, rapidly
obliterating landmark locations and any memory of where and how these now
established genres came into being.
If we are lucky, decades later some intrepid explorers come along. The young,
passionate, and curious to see for themselves how so much creative force burst
into life in these humble precincts. Ciro Frank Schiappa and Michele Primi,
two young Italians, took it upon themselves to do the urban anthropology required
to dig out the story of where rock was born in the New York City of the 1960s
carrying around an old Deardorff, 8 x 10 inch, wooden view camera.
Ciro, the photographer of this duo, used this extraordinary instrument to align
the legends of history with the current reality of the neighborhoods where
the story of rock was made. The precision of his descriptions of place allow us
to stare at these rude dwellings and storefronts, and now the modern ruin that has
replaced them, and wonder "what was it *there*" that allowed Patti Smith,
Leonard Cohen, or Iggy Pop to find their sound, their voice, their sweet,
risk-taking courage to bring their music out into the world.
Michele, the storyteller, has kept a running commentary of lives lived and music
made in these now quiet streets. He does so without sentiment or romance,
and has the courage to let the wonder of the past stand as it was.
We don't see, among the addresses pictured here, anything from the Upper
East Side, Fifth Avenue, Central Park West, or Sutton Place. No, the energy was
Downtown, and out in the 'nabes. Today, the Downtown scene is being pushed,
once again by financial pressure, further out into the far reaches of Brooklyn
and Queens.
Who knows what is on the horizon, and where it will put down its first roots?

New York Serenade provides a glimpse of New York through its music,
the evolution of its urban architecture, and the changing face of the metropolis.
These forty-eight photographs on large-format (8 x 10 inch) plates transform
a series of places that have gone down in the annals of New York rock into
modern-day icons.
The dialogue between the traditional and the contemporary maps out an itinerary
with places that may be nothing much to look at today, but which have played host
to crucial moments in the development of modern rock culture: a storefront, a table
in a diner, buildings and intersections that have become symbolic, apartments
where songs were written that encapsulate a moment in time, legendary venues
that no longer exist.
The streets of New York tell rock 'n' roll stories, and to revisit them through
analogue photography is to re-live the passion and the madness, the innocence
and the degradation, the desire to make it and the creative frenzy of the artists
who have left an indelible mark on the cultural life of the city. Debbie Harry would
make her way right across New York, from Manhattan to Sheepshead Bay,
the last exit to Brooklyn, to see punk band The Dictators and their incredible
frontman, "Handsome Dick" Manitoba; The Ramones came from Queens
to the Bowery, setting up their headquarters in the loft of Mexican artist Arturo
Vega; and Bob Dylan went all the way to the swamps of Mermaid Avenue
to search for the lost songs of his hero, Woody Guthrie.
We walked the same streets, inspired by the poetry and the sense of wonder
of "New York City Serenade," a song by Bruce Springsteen.
New York Serenade tells a tale that spans from the 1970s into the new
millennium—one that will perhaps never end—through different music genres
and generations, to celebrate a past that is fading but not forgotten . . . while
somewhere else, in an as-yet-undiscovered corner of the city, the future
of rock 'n' roll is being born.

On July 2, 1966 Keith Richard's girlfriend, Linda Keith, compelled
all the members of The Rolling Stones to come and see an
unknown guitarist named Jimi Hendrix performing with The Blue
Flames at Ondine, a club on East 59th Street, just beneath the
Queensboro Bridge.

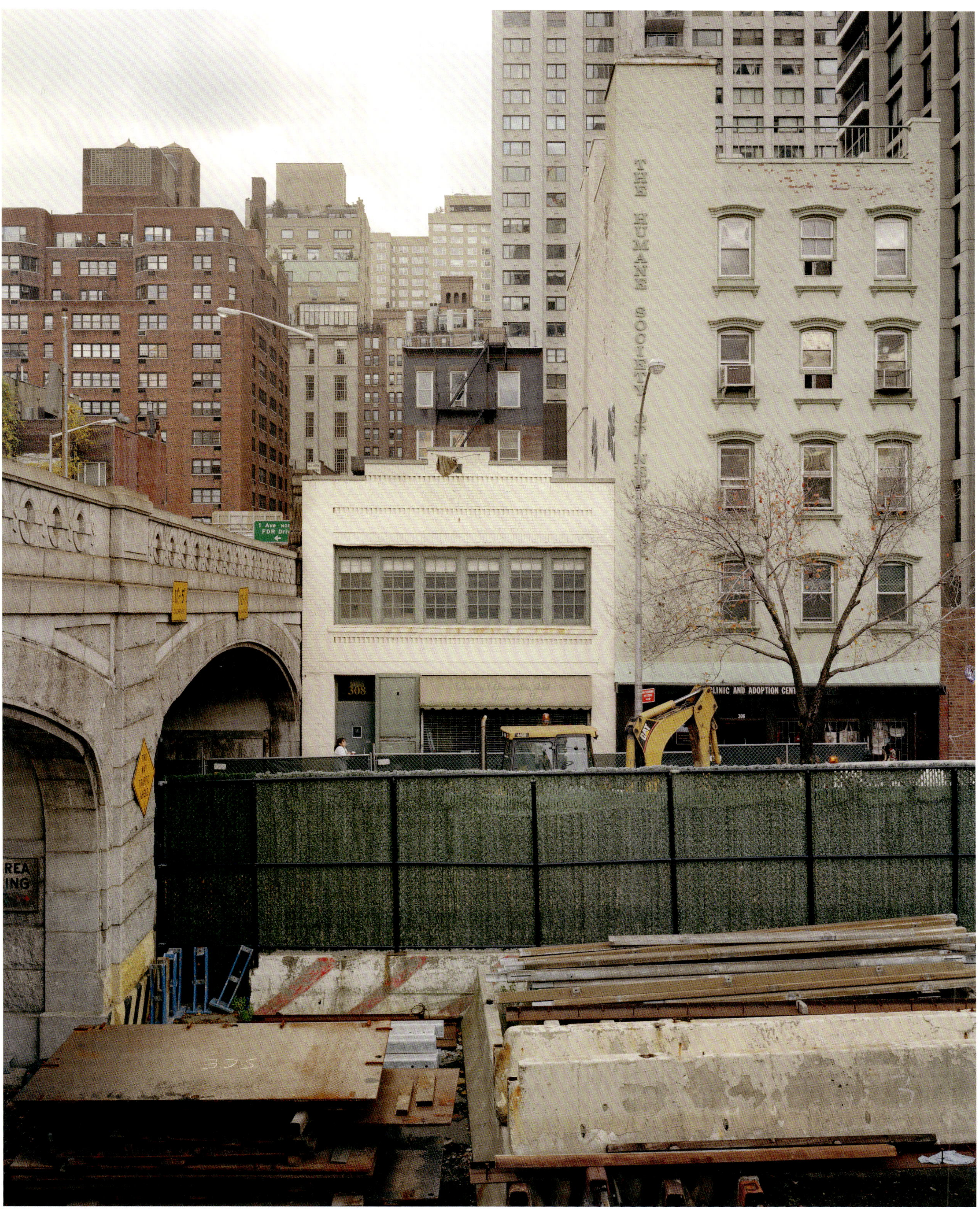

On July 4, 1976 The Ramones played their very first
gig outside America at the Roundhouse in London.
They were booked as the opening act of a veteran
San Francisco band, Flaming Groovies. Their set started
with "Loudmouth" and ended seventeen songs later
with a cover of "Let's Dance." It was the spark that
triggered the punk revolution in the UK.
Right before leaving America for the first time in his life,
Joey Ramone had taken his passport photo standing
with his back on the bathroom door of Arturo Vega's loft
on East 2nd and Bowery.

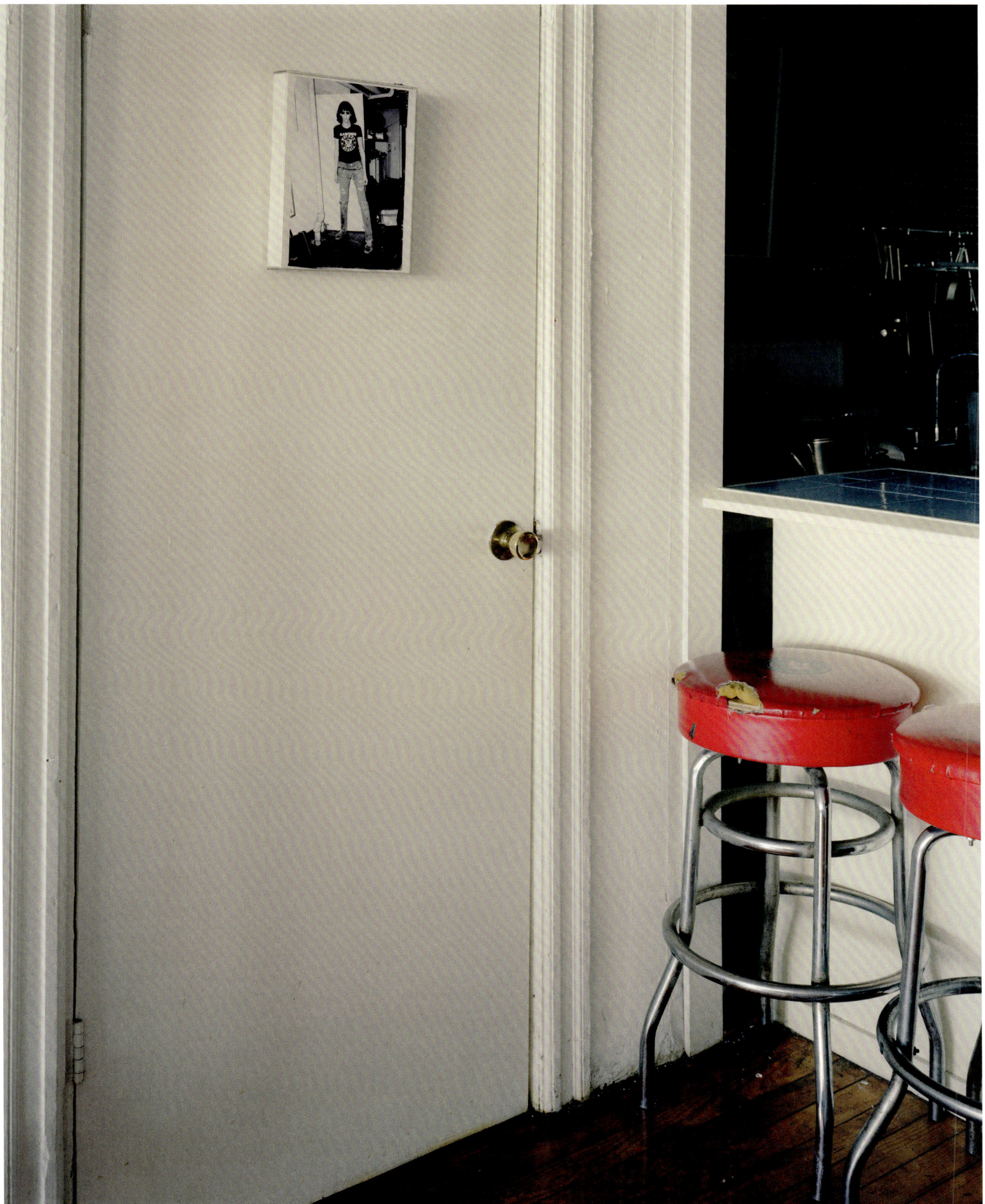

Christodora House is a building located at 143 Avenue B.
It was built in 1928 as a settlement house for low-income
and immigrant residents, providing food, shelter, and health
services. It is believed that in the 1960s, the national
headquarters of the Black Panthers was located
in the building, and that it was also the site of several
pornographic movies.
In 1986, Christodora House was turned into a condominium
for the new residents of the Lower East Side. Iggy Pop
was one of the first to buy an apartment here, where
he wrote the songs on his twelfth album, "Avenue B."

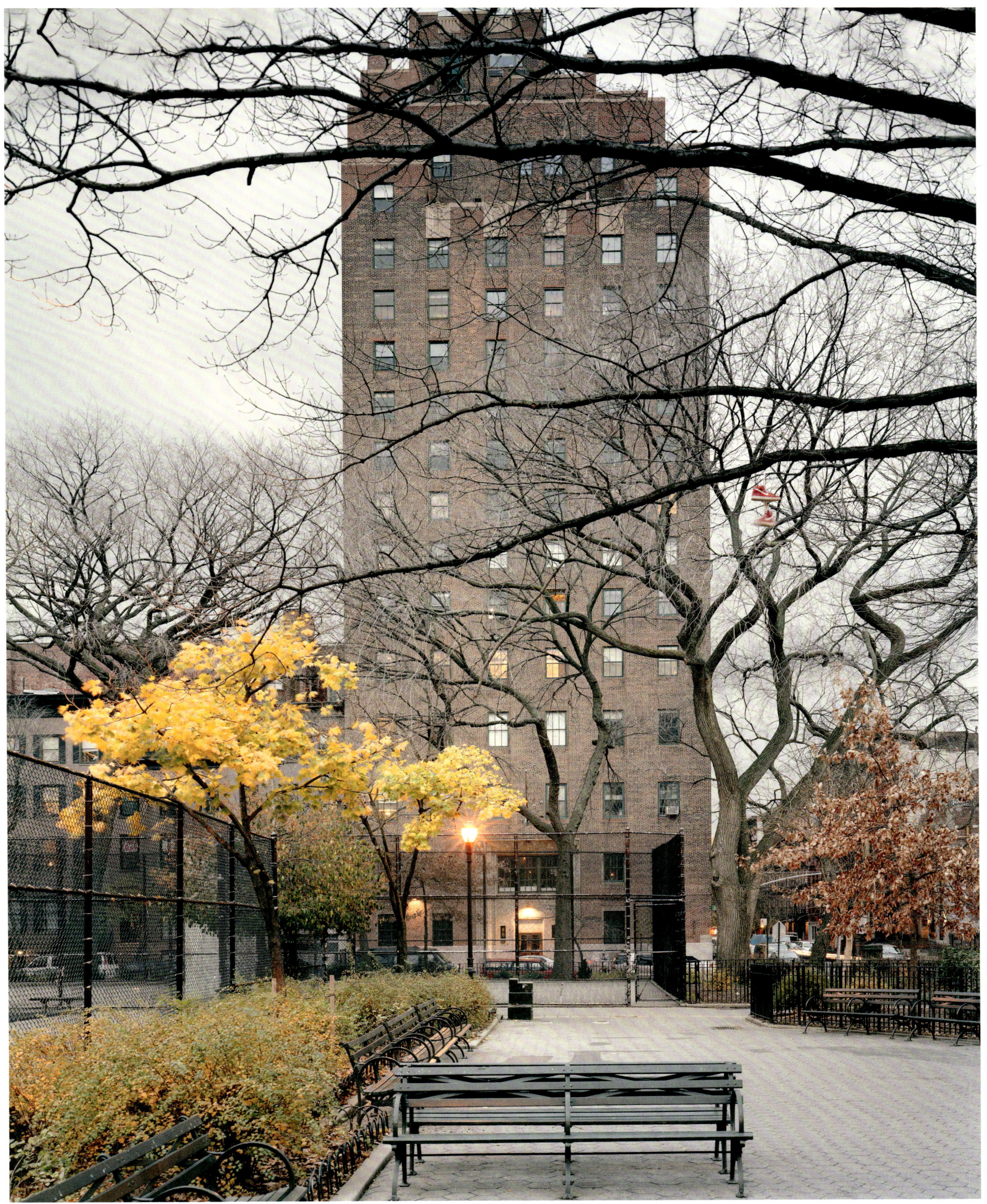

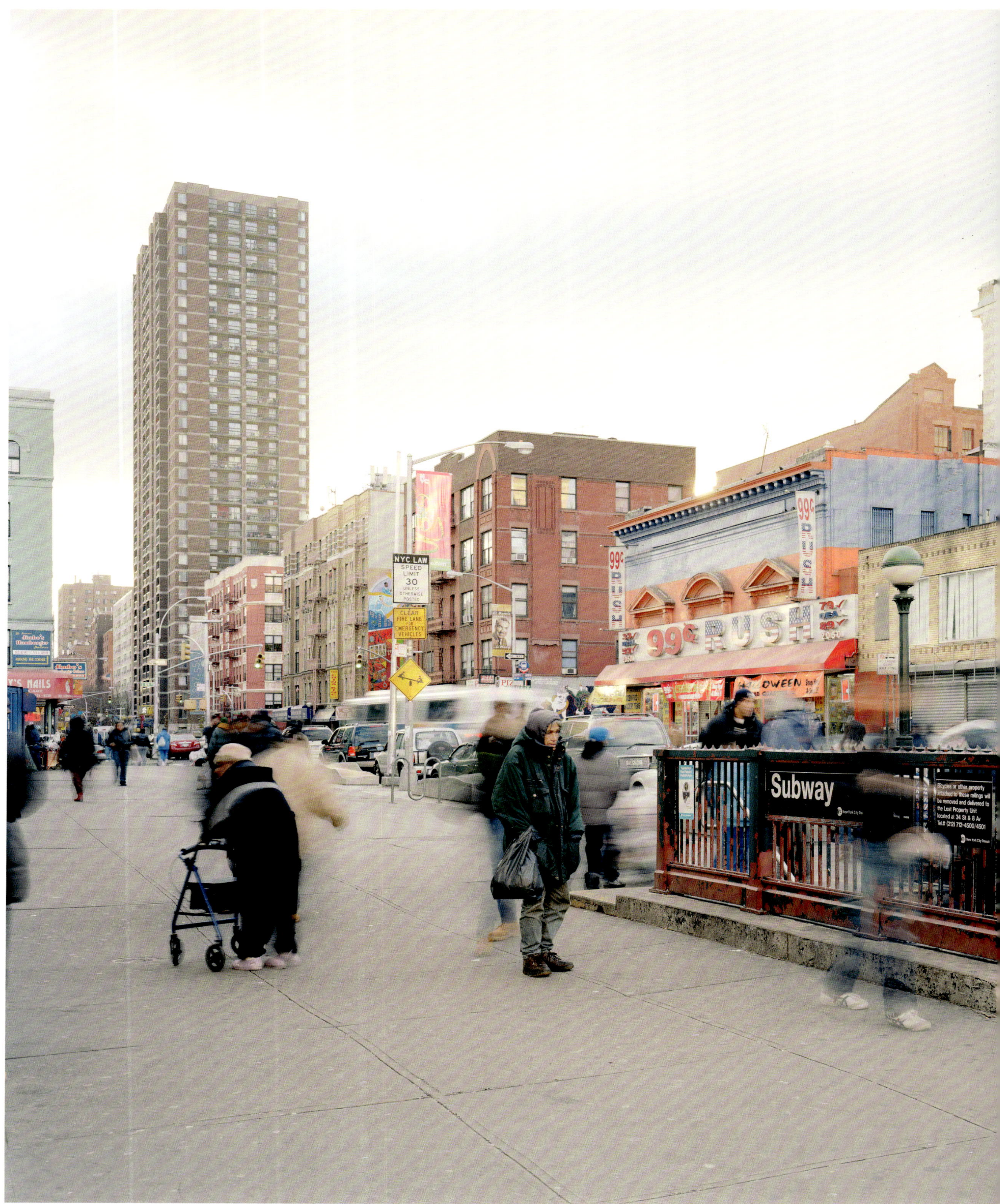
NYC LAW
SPEED
LIMIT
30
UNLESS
OTHERWISE
POSTED
CLEAR
FIRE LANE
EMERGENCY
VEHICLES
99¢
99¢
99¢
99¢
RUSH
HALLOWEEN
Subway
New York City Transit
Bicycles or other property
attached to these railings will
be removed and delivered to
the Lost Property Unit
located at 34 St & 8 Av
Tel.# (212) 712-4500/4501
'S NAILS

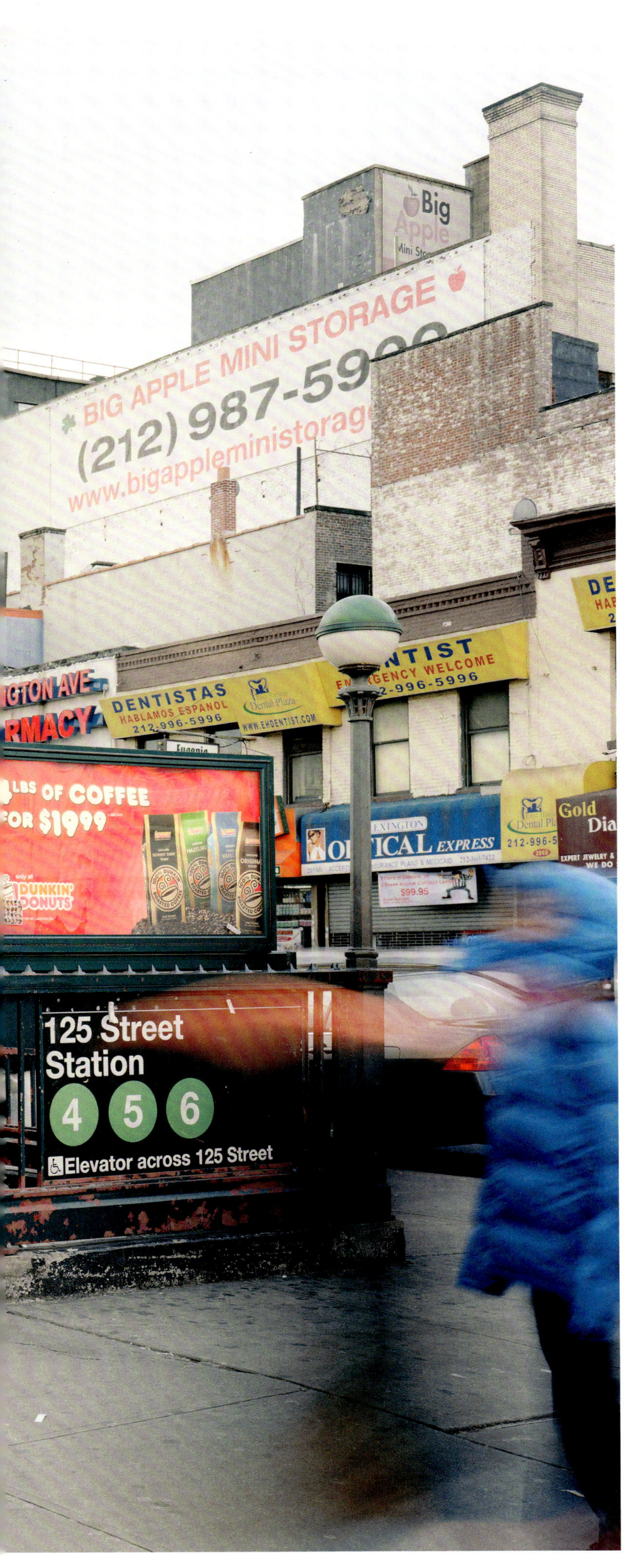

In the early 1960s, while he was still a student
at Syracuse University, Lou Reed wrote a song describing
a trip to a Harlem brownstone at the intersection
of Lexington Avenue and 125th Street to buy 26 dollars
worth of heroin from a dealer, "the man."
"I'm Waiting For The Man" was one of the first songs
he recorded with John Cale and Sterling Morrison.
It was released in March 1967 on the debut album
of The Velvet Underground.
Lou Reed once said that everything about that song
is true, except the price.

Photographer Peter Corriston was looking for a building
that was symmetrical with interesting details to shoot
the cover of Led Zeppelin's sixth record, "Physical Graffiti."

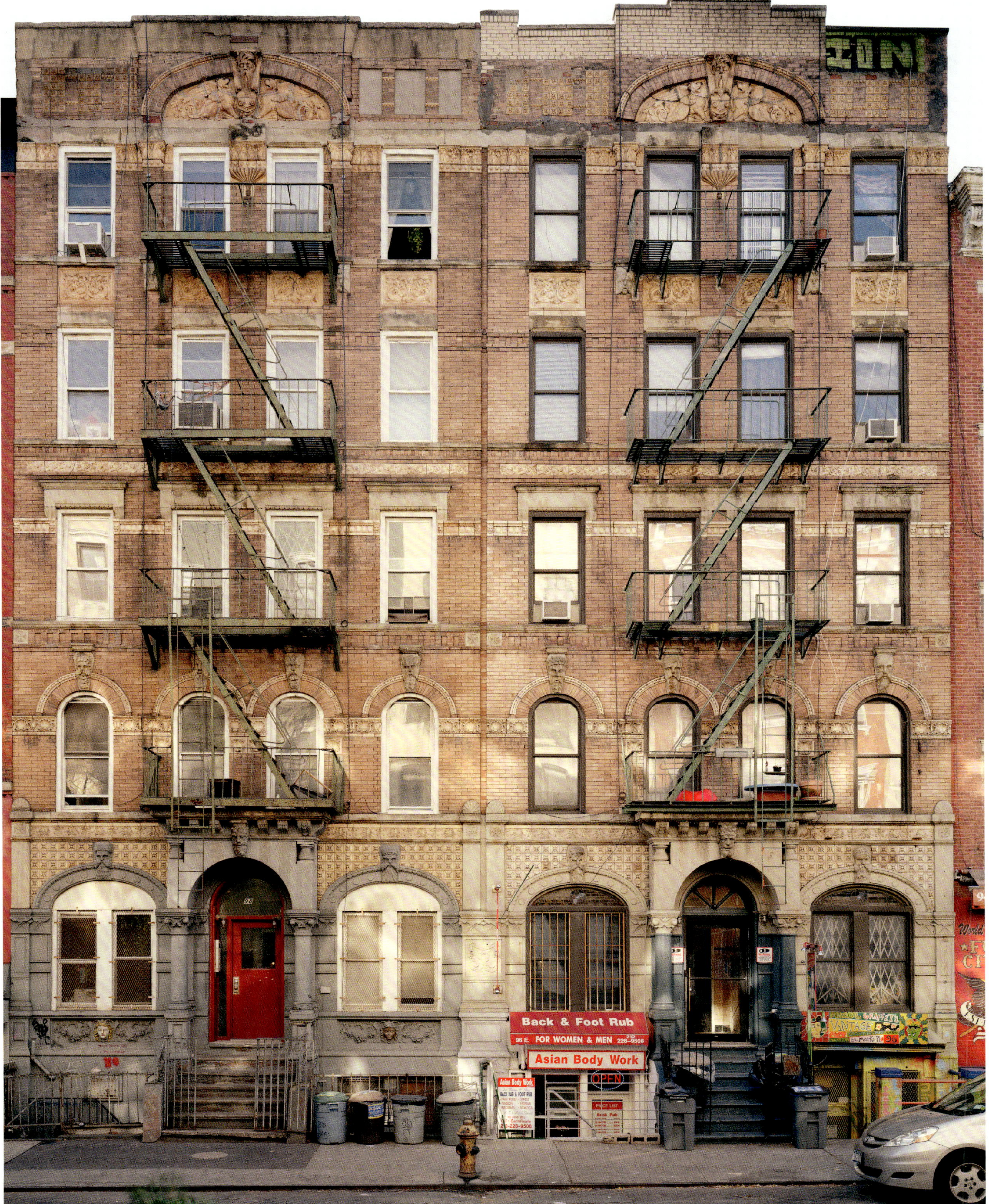
Back & Foot Rub
96 E.   FOR WOMEN & MEN   212 228-9508
Asian Body Work
OPEN
Asian Body Work
BACK RUB & FOOT RUB
PAIN RELIEF • STRESS
TENSION • FATIGUE
INSOMNIA • SCIATICA
WE ALSO SELL
Gift Certificate
212-228-9508
PRICE LIST
Back Rub
VANTAGE

In 1974, Leonard Cohen wrote a song about meeting
a famous singer in an elevator of the Chelsea Hotel and
having sex with her.
The song is "Chelsea Hotel #2."
He later admitted that it was about Janis Joplin.

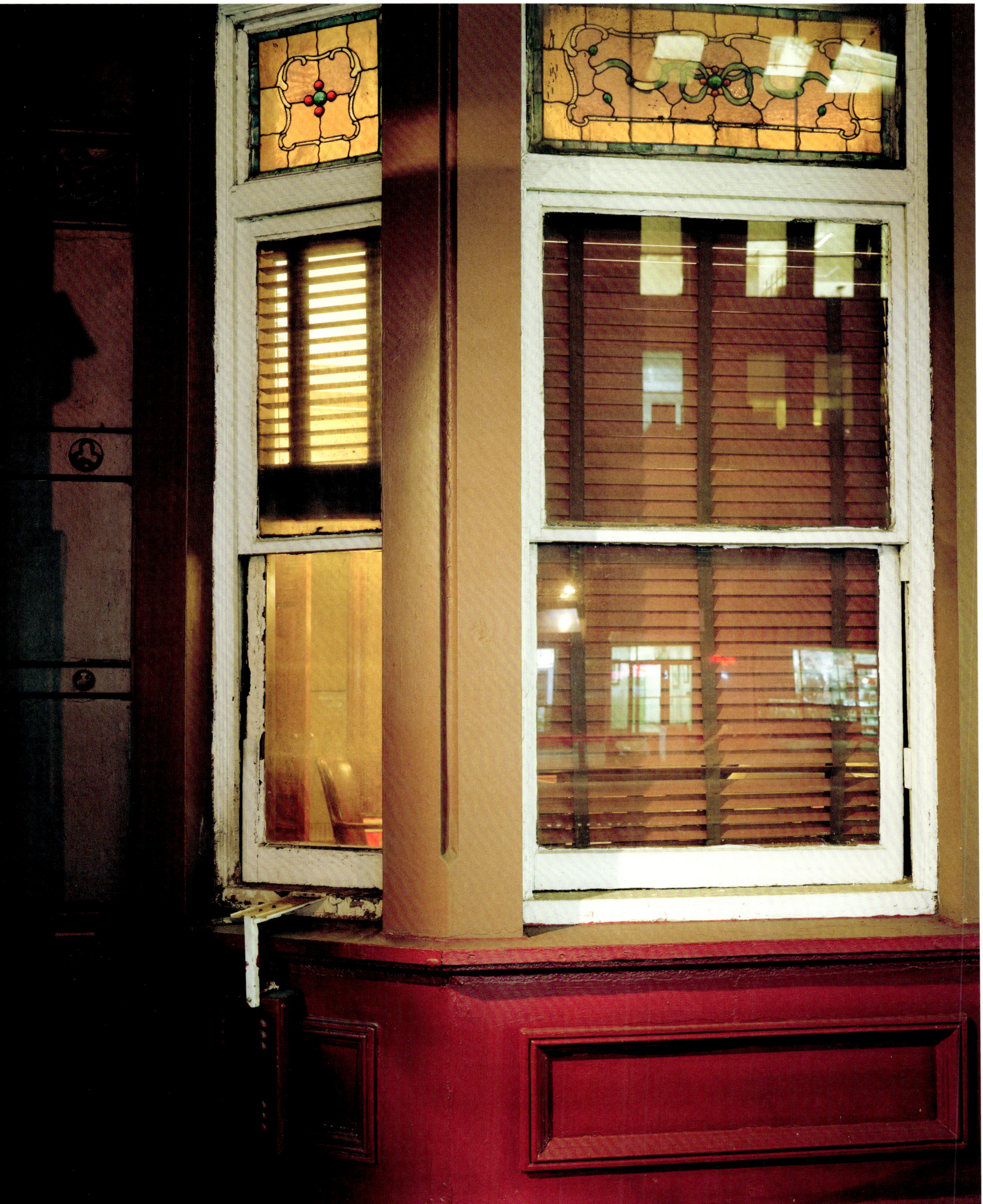

"New York City Serenade" is the last track on Bruce
Springsteen's second album, "The Wild, The Innocent
& The E Street Shuffle" released on September 11, 1973.
It evolved from "Vibes Man," one of the songs Springsteen
played at his Colombia Records audition with talent scout
John Hammond in May 1972.
It tells the story of Billy and Diamond Jackie, a couple
of young and wild New Jersey kids who travel to Manhattan
and walk down Broadway at night in search of their love.

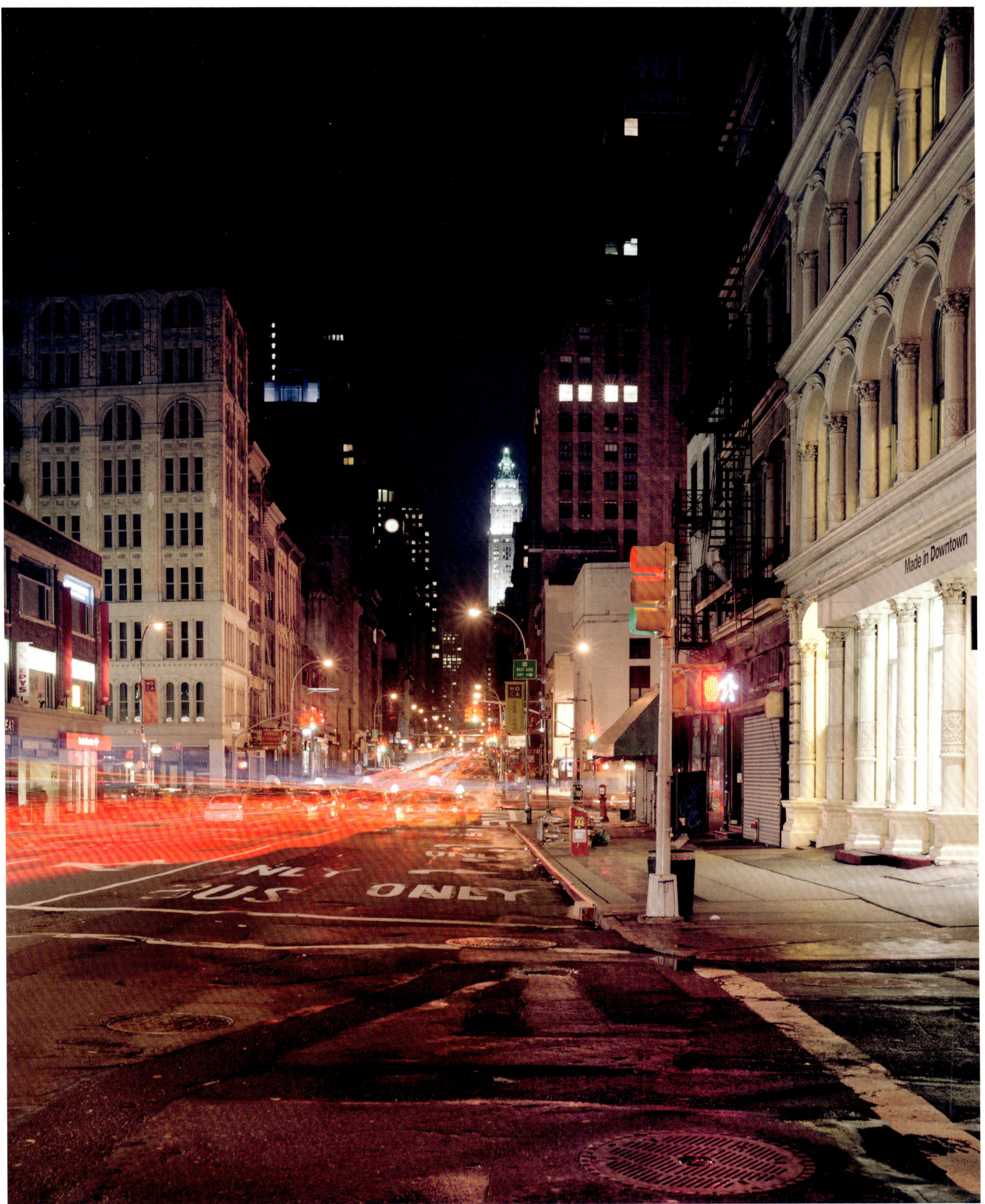
401
Made in Downtown
MOCA
BUS ONLY
ONLY

Patti Smith and Robert Mapplethorpe were looking for
a place to live when they found an apartment in a three-story
red brick building at 160 Hall Street in Brooklyn.
They were both young, hungry, and ready to develop
their artistic talents. The apartment was in dire conditions,
but the rent was just 80 dollars a month. So they moved
there in 1967.

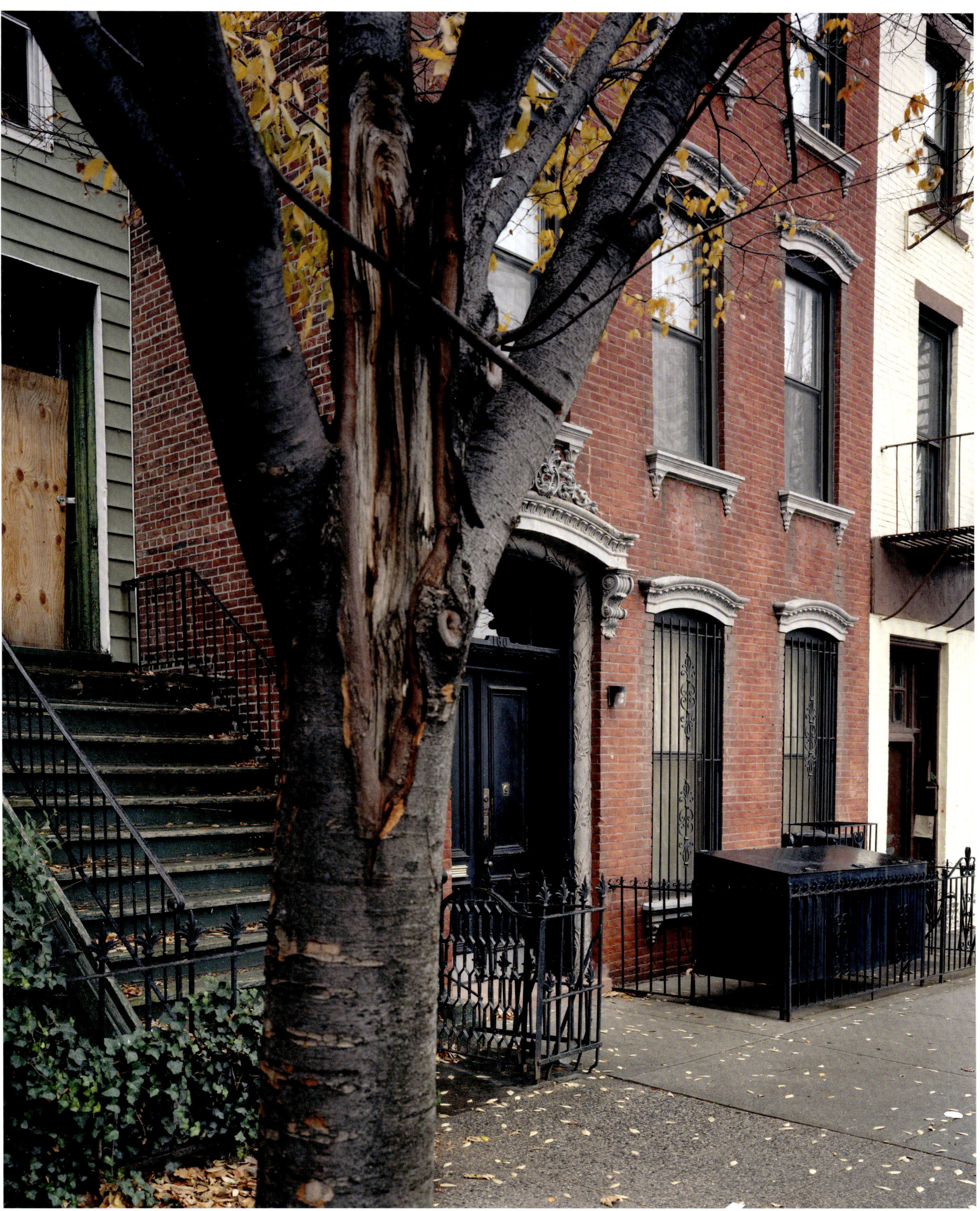

In 1981, David Byrne from Talking Heads came up
with the idea for a song about not being happy with the
things you have. He later explained that he wrote
the lyrics based on words from the sermons of evangelist
preachers he recorded off the radio.
The song was "Once In A Lifetime."

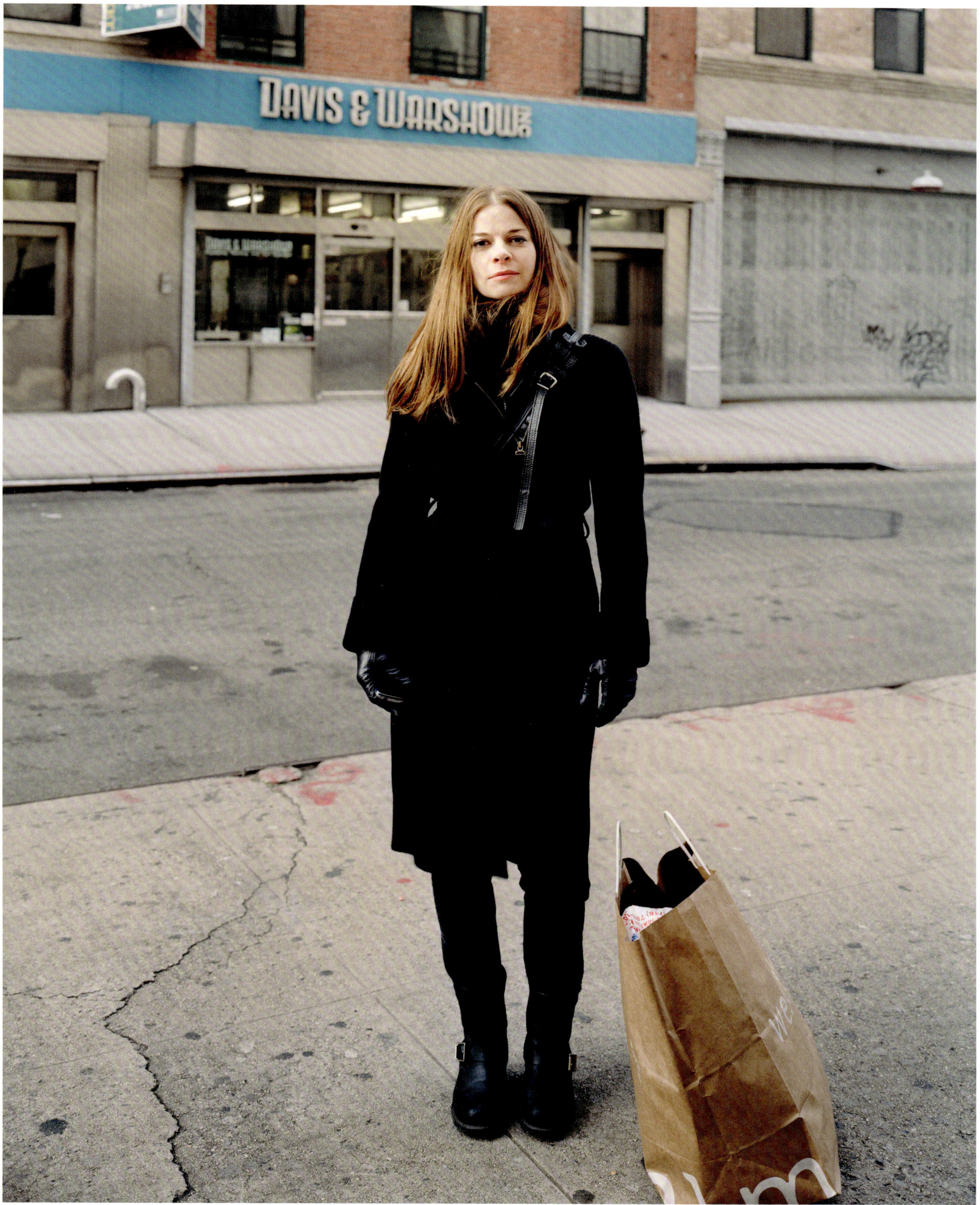

DAVIS & WARSHOW

When police entered Tonic Club at 107 Norfolk Street
at 4:30 am on Friday, April 13, 2007, jazz guitarist
Marc Ribot kept on playing the alltime classic by Glenn
Miller, "Nearness of You."
He was handcuffed and led outside along with activist
Rebecca Moore, founder of "Take It to the Bridge,"
an association concerned with safeguarding the creative
and cultural heritage of New York and struggling against
rising rents and the gentrification of the Lower East Side.

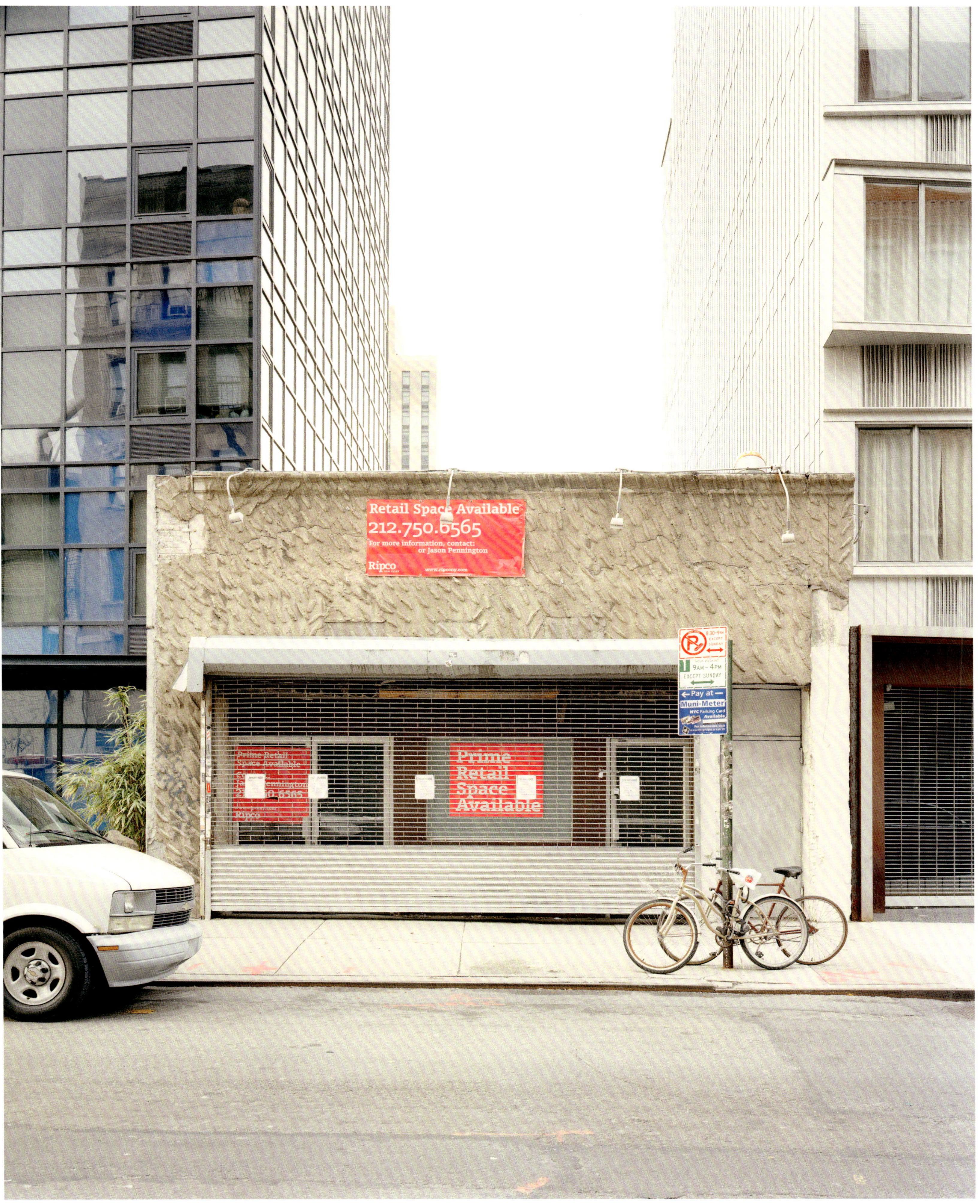

Retail Space Available
212.750.6565
For more information, contact:
or Jason Pennington
Ripco
www.ripcony.com
Prime Retail
Space Available
Pennington
6565
Ripco
Prime
Retail
Space
Available
9 AM – 4 PM
EXCEPT SUNDAY
Pay at
Muni-Meter
NYC Parking Card
Available

Ohio-born indie band The National had established
themselves permanently in Ditmas Park, Brooklyn,
when Matt Berninger wrote the lyrics of "Daughters
of the SoHo Riots."
Before moving to Brooklyn, Matt had shared a studio
apartment with three other people sleeping on the floor
in sleeping bags on East 60th, right underneath
the Queensboro Bridge. "Daughters of the SoHo Riots"
was released in 2005 on their third album, "Alligator."
It was the album that established The National as one
of the best bands of the year.
Matt Berninger said about New York: "It's a muse,
and it's a fantasy place. It's just such a romantic strange
city that's always a part of the songs."

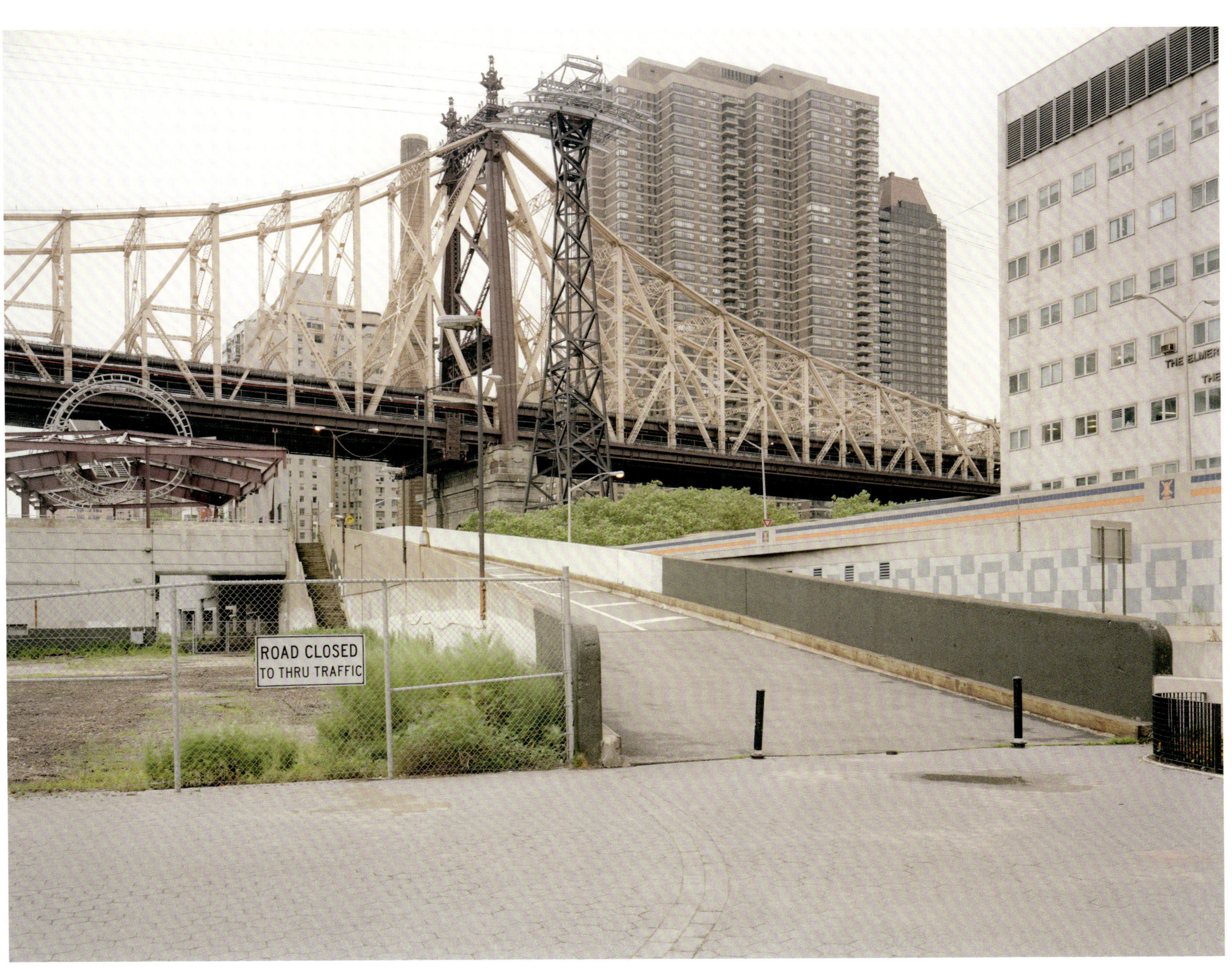

ROAD CLOSED
TO THRU TRAFFIC

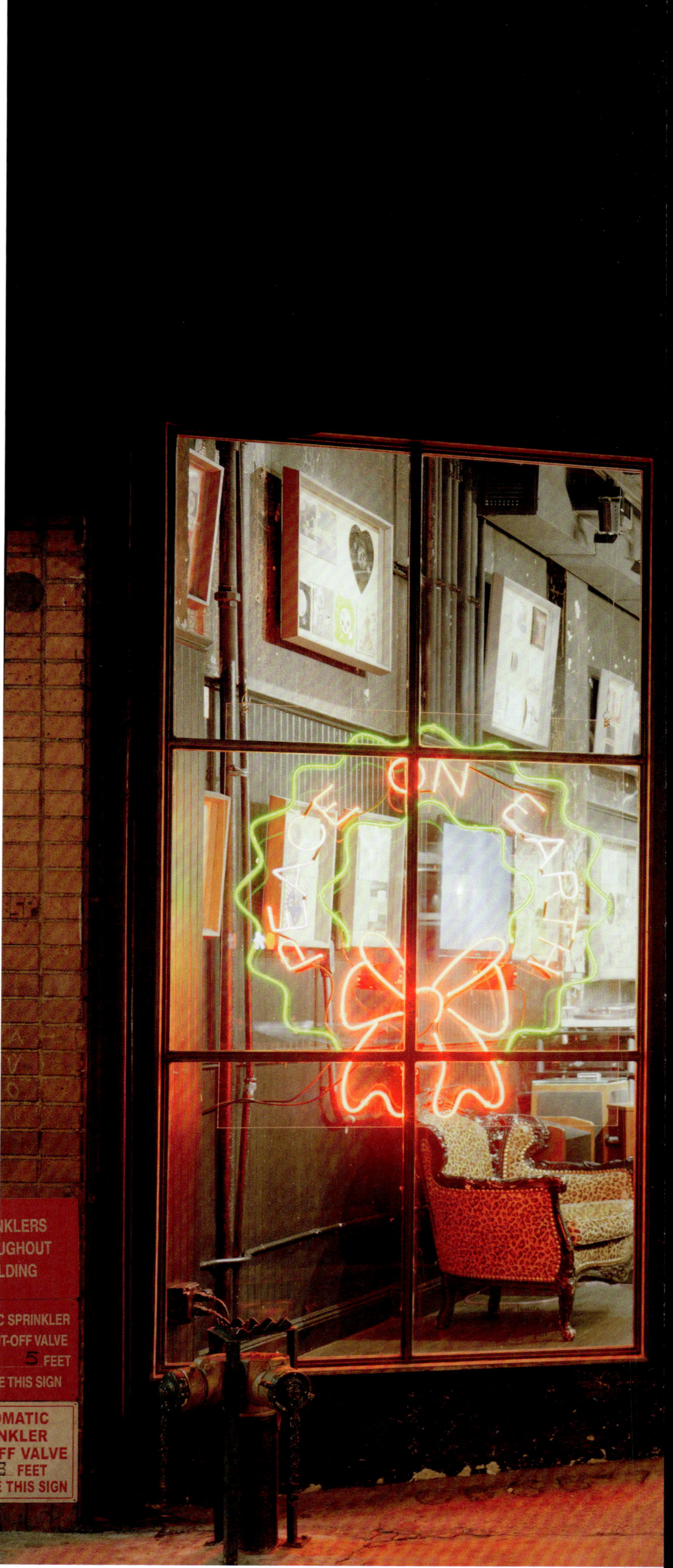

In 1974, Tom Verlaine was looking for a venue for his
band, Television, when he found a place at 315 Bowery,
right below one of New York's largest flophouses for the
homeless, known as The Palace Hotel.
The owner, Hilly Kristal, had just reopened and was on
a ladder hanging the new sign: CBGB. When Tom Verlaine
asked him what the letters meant, he answered: "Country,
bluegrass, blues."
None of these were ever played at CBGB.
It became, as Hilly Kristal himself said: "A place where
people could express frustrations, desires, anxieties,
and maybe even dreams."

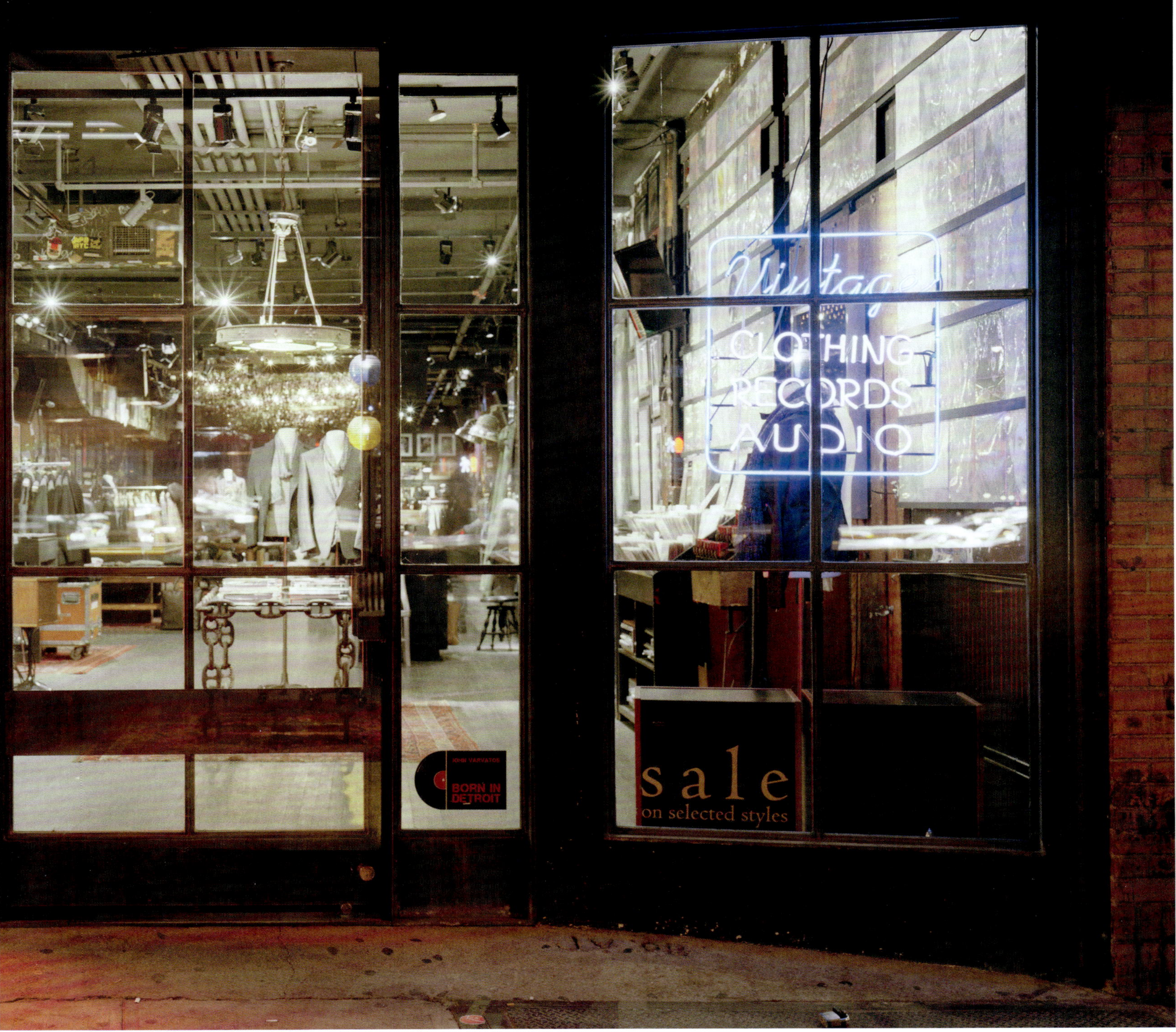
ohn varvatos
315 Bowery
Vintage
CLOTHING
RECORDS
AUDIO
JOHN VARVATOS
BORN IN DETROIT
sale
on selected styles

In 1989, Shane Doyle and Karl Geary opened a cafe
at 122 St. Mark's Place, soon to become the hangout
for the younger generation of Irish immigrants who
came to New York in the 1980s from a recession-dimmed
Ireland. Upcoming artists like Ben Folds and David Gray
took their first steps in the music business playing for tips,
while established acts like Sinéad O'Connor, Shane
MacGowan, and Waterboys performed here everytime
they came to New York. In April 1992, a young boy took
the stage at Sin-é.
His name was Jeff Buckley.
He quickly earned a Monday-night slot and recorded
his first album, "Live at Sin-é," here. Sin-é closed in 1996.

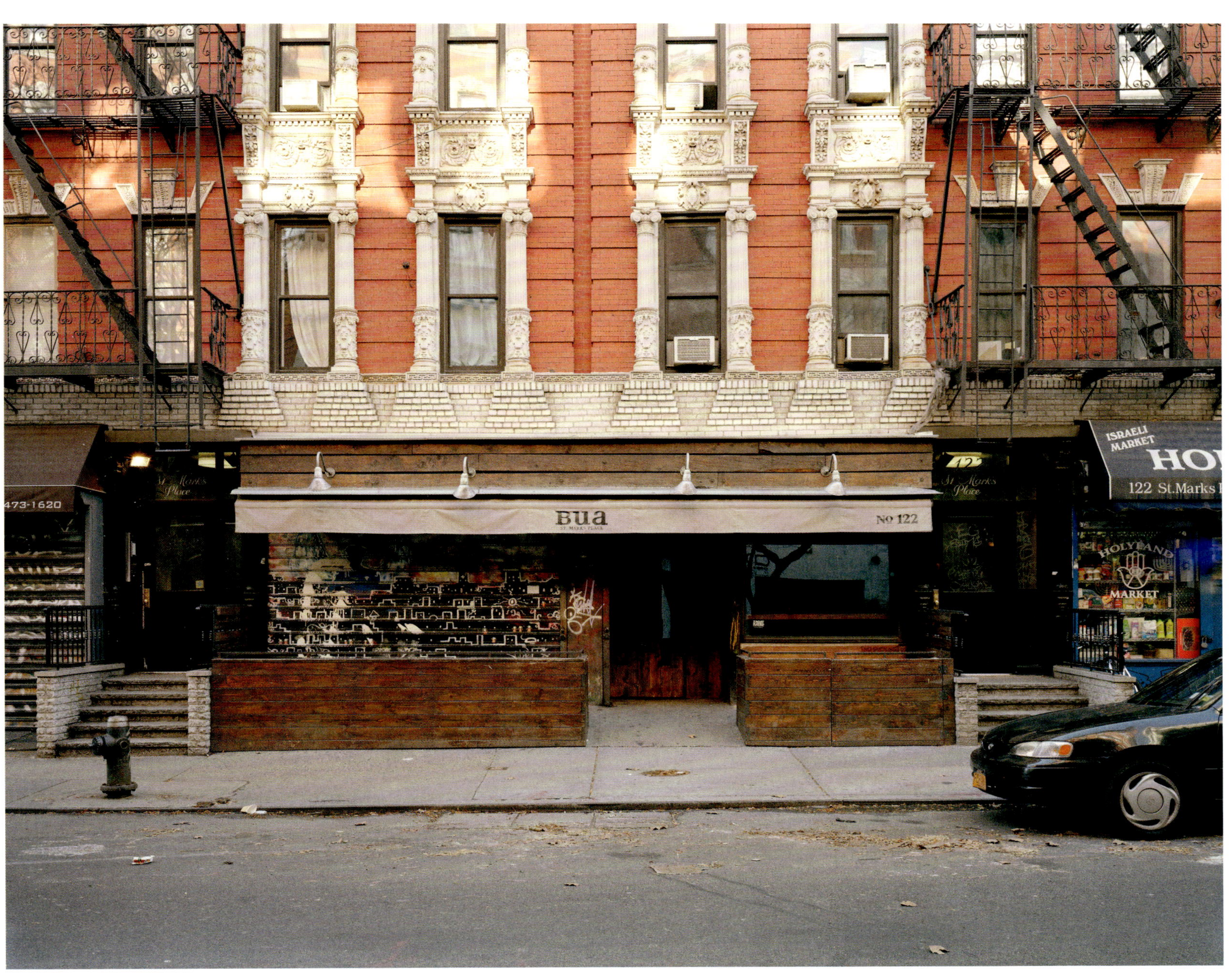
473-1620
St. Marks Place
BUA
ST. MARKS PLACE
No 122
ISRAELI MARKET
HO
122 St.Marks
St. Marks Place
HOLYLAND
MARKET

When James Brown arrived for the first time in New York
in April 1959, he headed straight for the Apollo Theater
in Harlem to see The Dells and The Cadillacs perform.
On October 24, 1962 he recorded, at his own expense,
his performance with The Famous Flames for the album
"Live at the Apollo."
Released in May 1963, it spent 66 weeks on the pop
album chart and peaked at number 2, starting a musical
revolution called funk.

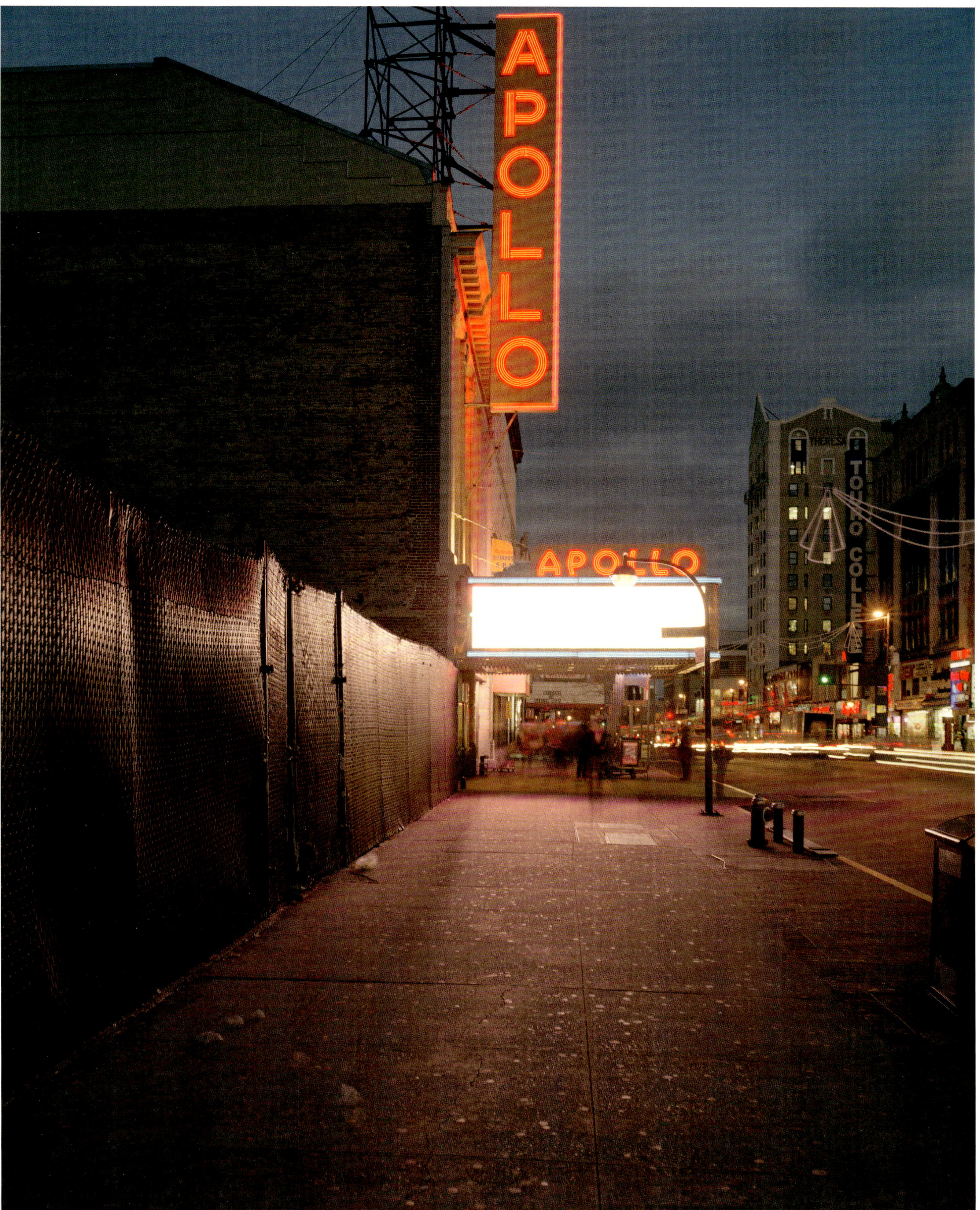

APOLLO
APOLLO
HOTEL THERESA
TOURO COLLE

Bob Dylan arrived in New York from the Midwest
in January 1961, after a twenty-four-hour ride in a four-door
'57 Impala sedan with fellow folksinger Fred Underhill
and a young couple.
He wanted to come to New York to find the singers
he had heard on the radio in his hometown Duluth,
in Minnesota: Dave Van Ronk, Pete Seeger, and especially
Woody Guthrie.
The car stopped at 42nd Street. Bob Dylan stepped out
and walked down to Washington Square Park, in the heart
of Greenwich Village.
It was the coldest winter in seventeen years.

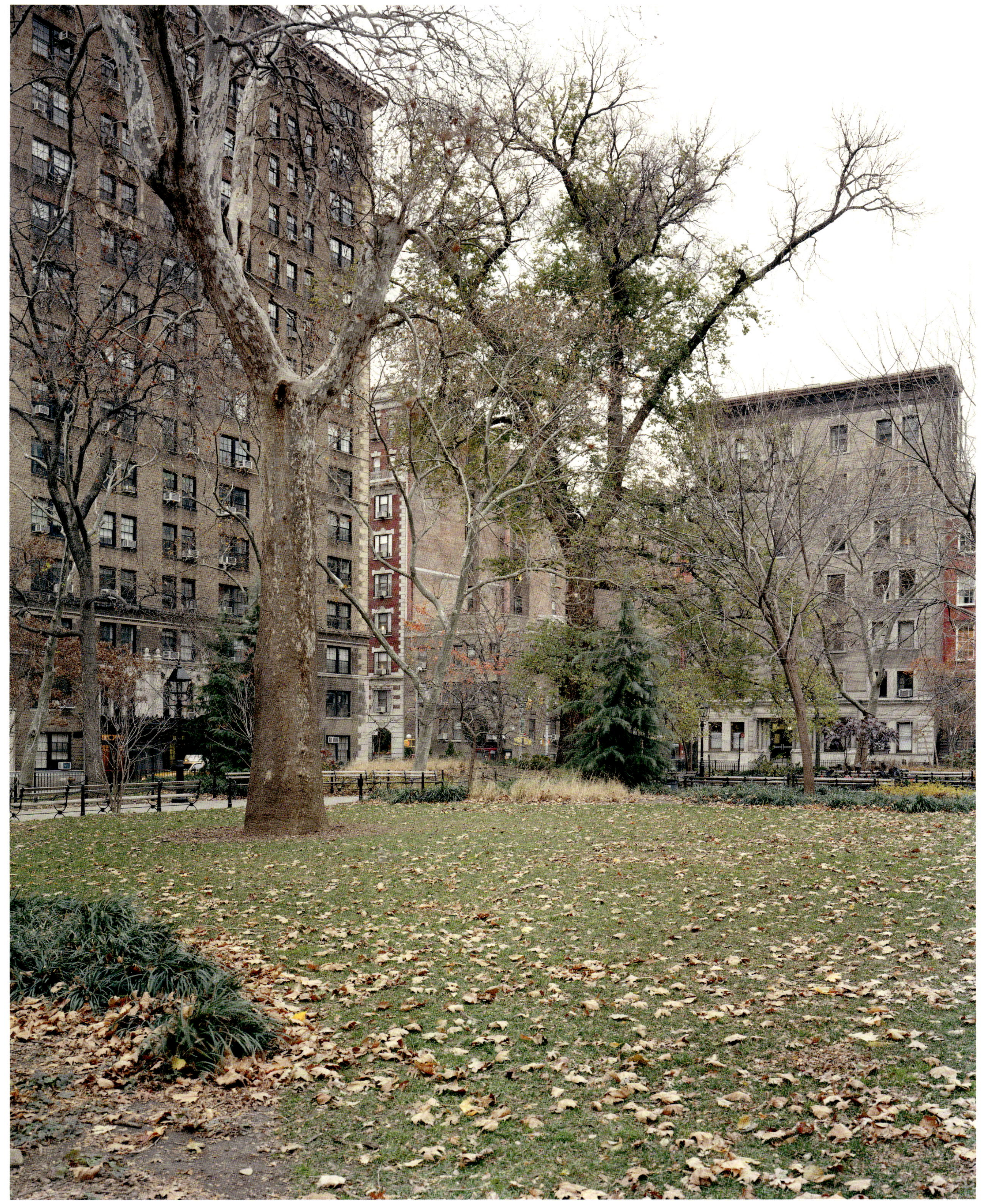

On August 13, 1975, Bruce Springsteen began
a five-night ten-show stand at The Bottom Line club on
15 West 4th Street to showcase his third album,
"Born To Run." It was the turning point of his career.
In 2003, the landlord of The Bottom Line—New York
University—raised the rent of the club to market level.
Bruce Springsteen offered to pay the club's back rent
if they could settle a lease.
The Bottom Line closed on January 22, 2004.

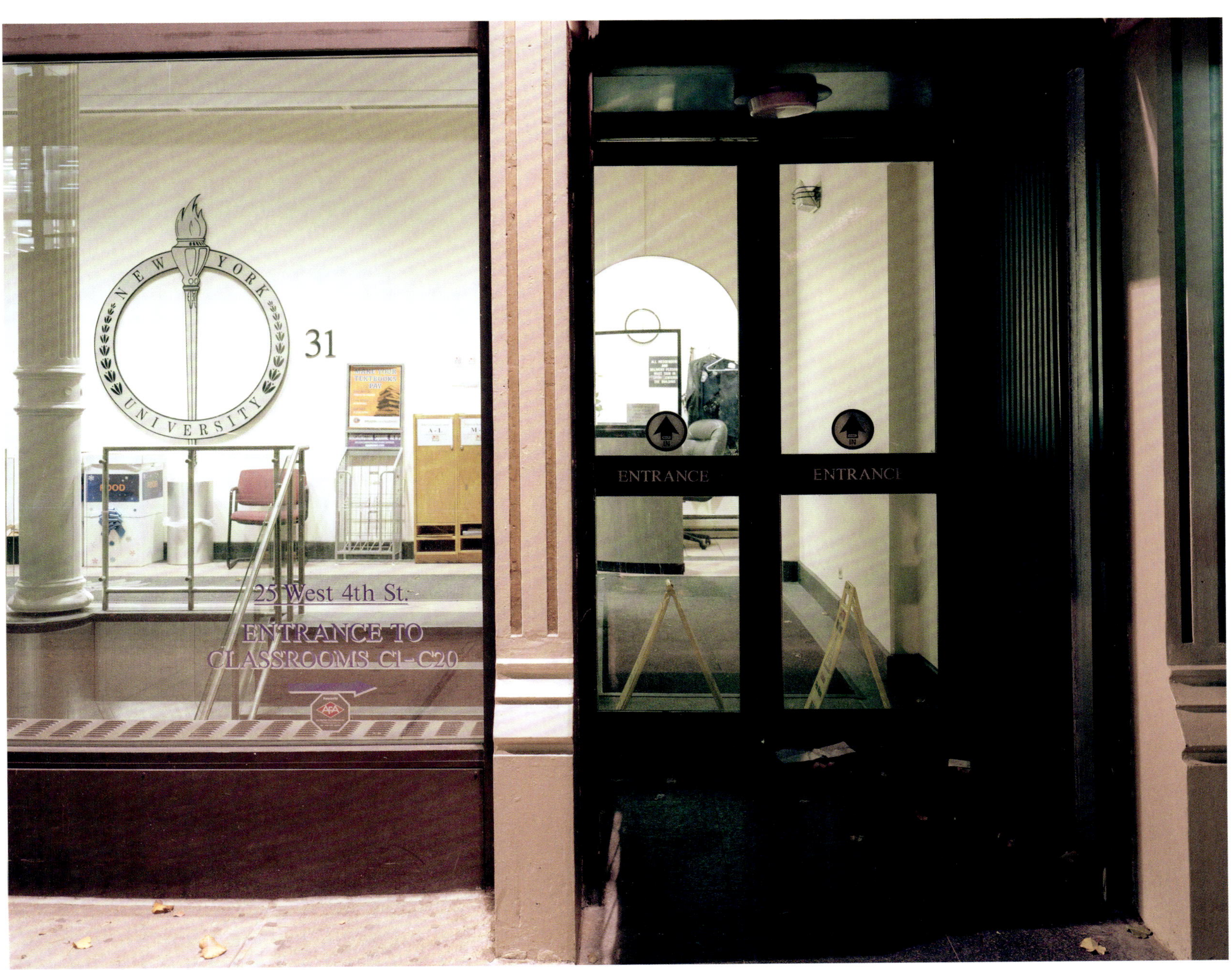
NEW YORK
UNIVERSITY
31
25 West 4th St.
ENTRANCE TO
CLASSROOMS C1-C20
ENTRANCE
ENTRANCE

In 2000, the New York club scene was swept away
by a band playing a stripped-down version of guitar rock
that launched a garage-rock revival movement across
the globe. The name of the band was The Strokes.
By the end of the decade, the scene was already over.
In 2009, the lead singer of The Strokes, Julian Casablancas,
evoked it in his first solo album with a song titled "Ludlow
Street" dedicated to one of the most iconic streets on
the Lower East Side, a destination for music, art, decadence,
and nightlife lovers.

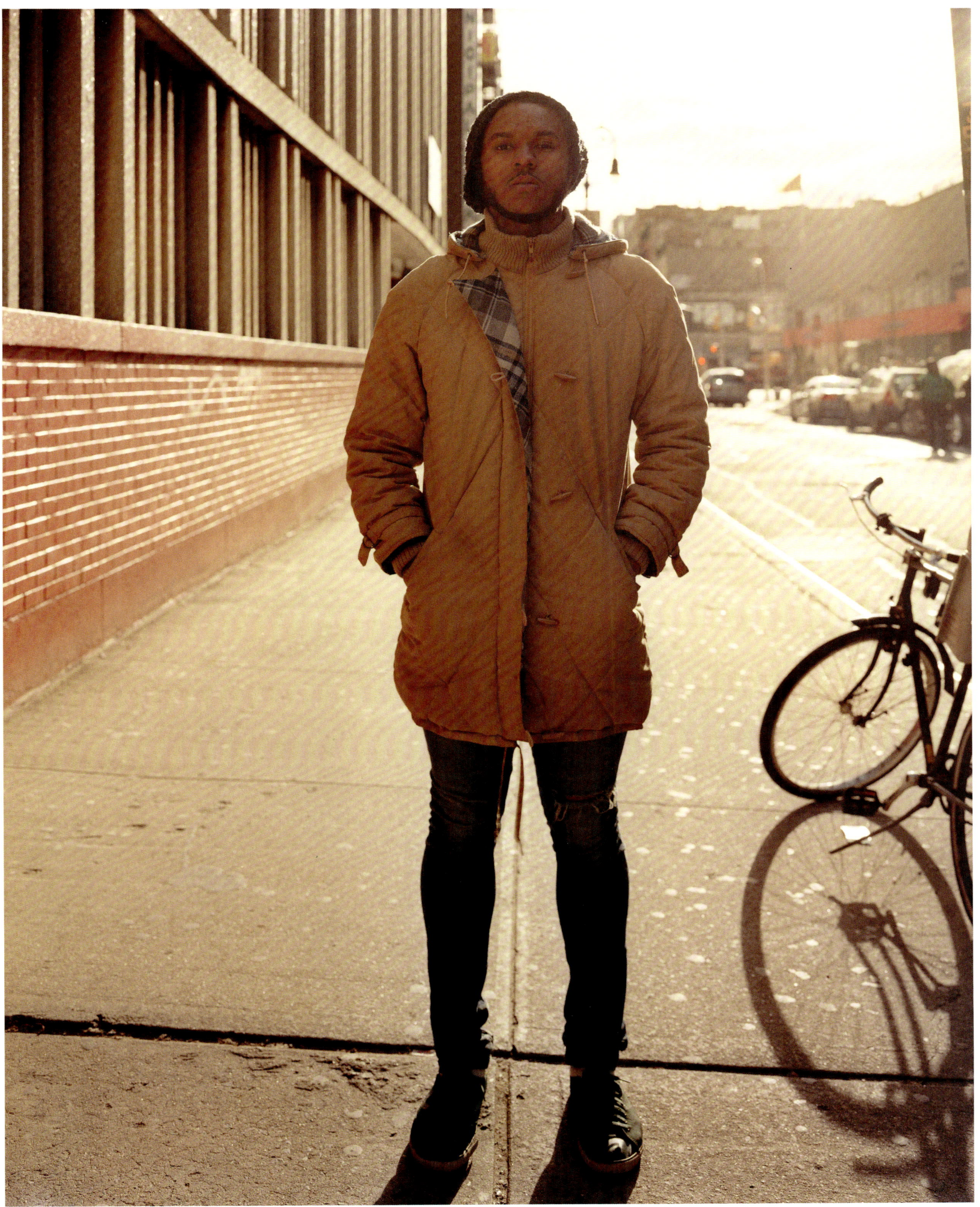

The first time the Beastie Boys earned any money was
in 1983 when they sued British Airways for using part
of their song "Beastie Revolution," released on the EP
"Cooky Puss," without their permission in a television ad.
They were given 40,000 dollars.
Mike D said that the money enabled the Beastie Boys
to make their move to independence: they rented an entire
floor in a "Chinese sweatshop building" at 59 Chrystie
Street. It became their home, rehearsing space, recording
studio, and party house.

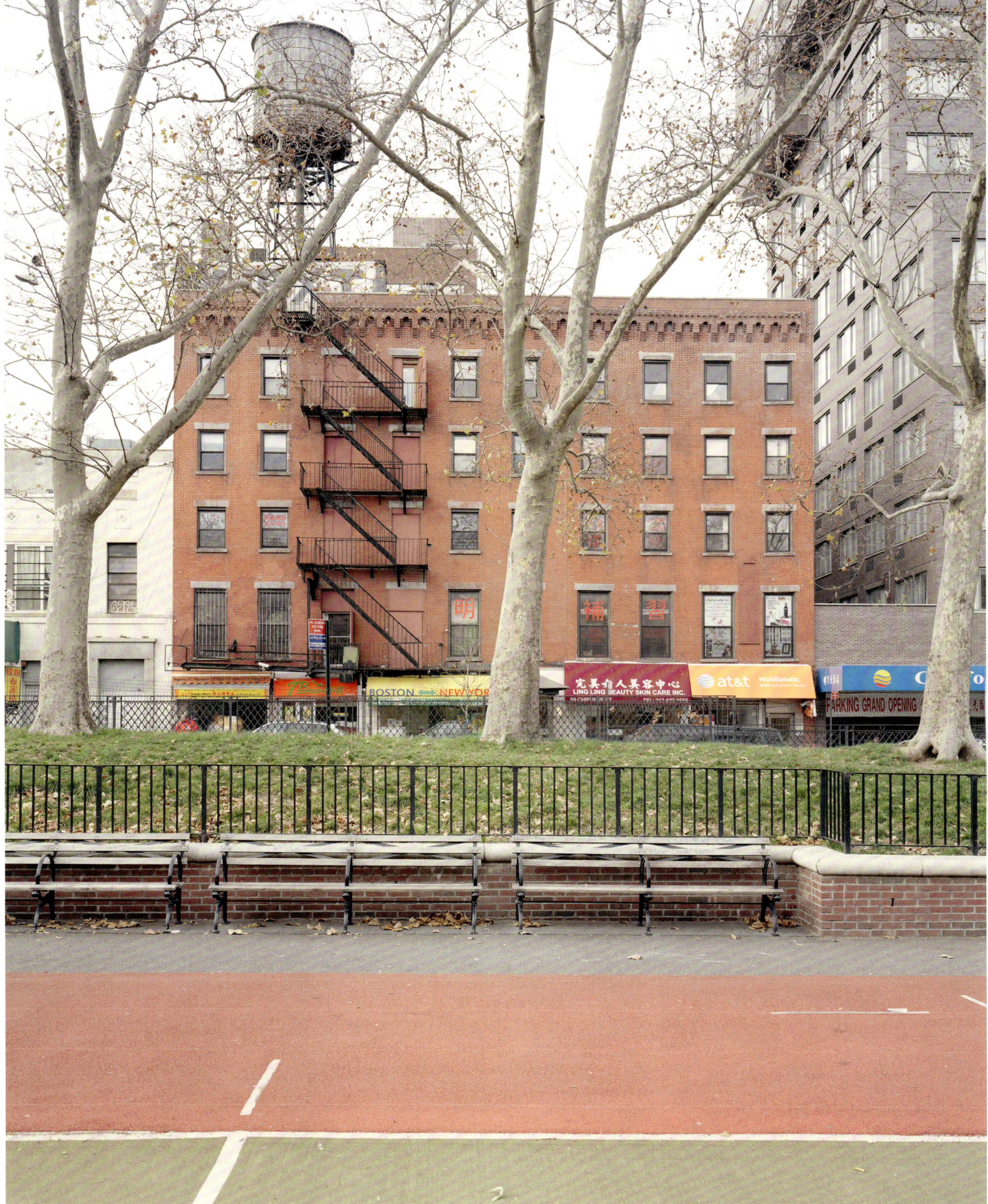
BOSTON ← → NEW YORK
完美佳人美容中心
LING LING BEAUTY SKIN CARE INC.
59 CHRYSTIE ST.   TEL 212-925-1655
at&t
Mobileistic
AT&T Authorized Reseller
PARKING GRAND OPENING
NO STANDING ANYTIME
明
補
智

In 1961, doo-wop sextet The Excellents, founded
by John and George Kuse, two brothers from the Bronx,
sang a ballad called "Coney Island Baby" dedicated
to a lovely hostess at Astroland Amusement Park.
It was released as the B-side of another single, but caught
the attention of radio deejays that began flipping the record
and playing it. It went to number 51 in the charts in 1962,
and became an all-time New York classic.
The Excellents were booked for a TV appareance
on "The Dick Clark Show" in Philadelphia, but when
John Kuse said they had no money and couldn't afford
to travel to Philly, their record company sent another band
under the same name.
The Excellents never recorded again.

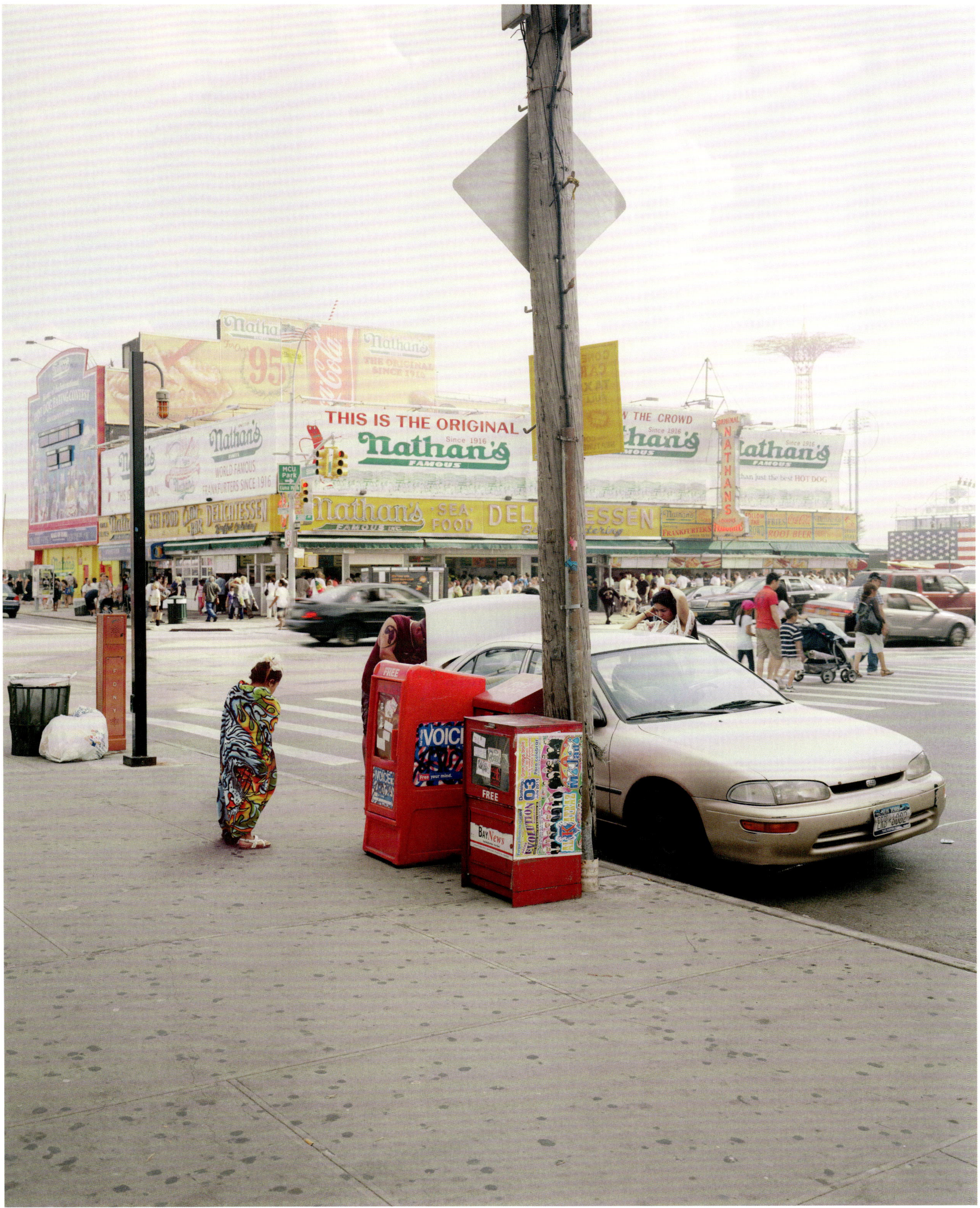

THIS IS THE ORIGINAL
Nathan's
Since 1916
FAMOUS
Nathan's
THE ORIGINAL
SINCE 1916
Coca-Cola
95
Nathan's
WORLD FAMOUS
FRANKFURTERS SINCE 1916
Nathan's
FAMOUS INC
SEA FOOD
DELICATESSEN
Nathan's
Since 1916
FAMOUS
ORIGINAL
NATHAN'S
than just the best HOT DOG
ROOT BEER
FRANKFURTERS
THE CROWD
MCU
Park
VOICE
FREE
Free your mind.
FREE
BayNews
EVOLUTION 03
FDNY

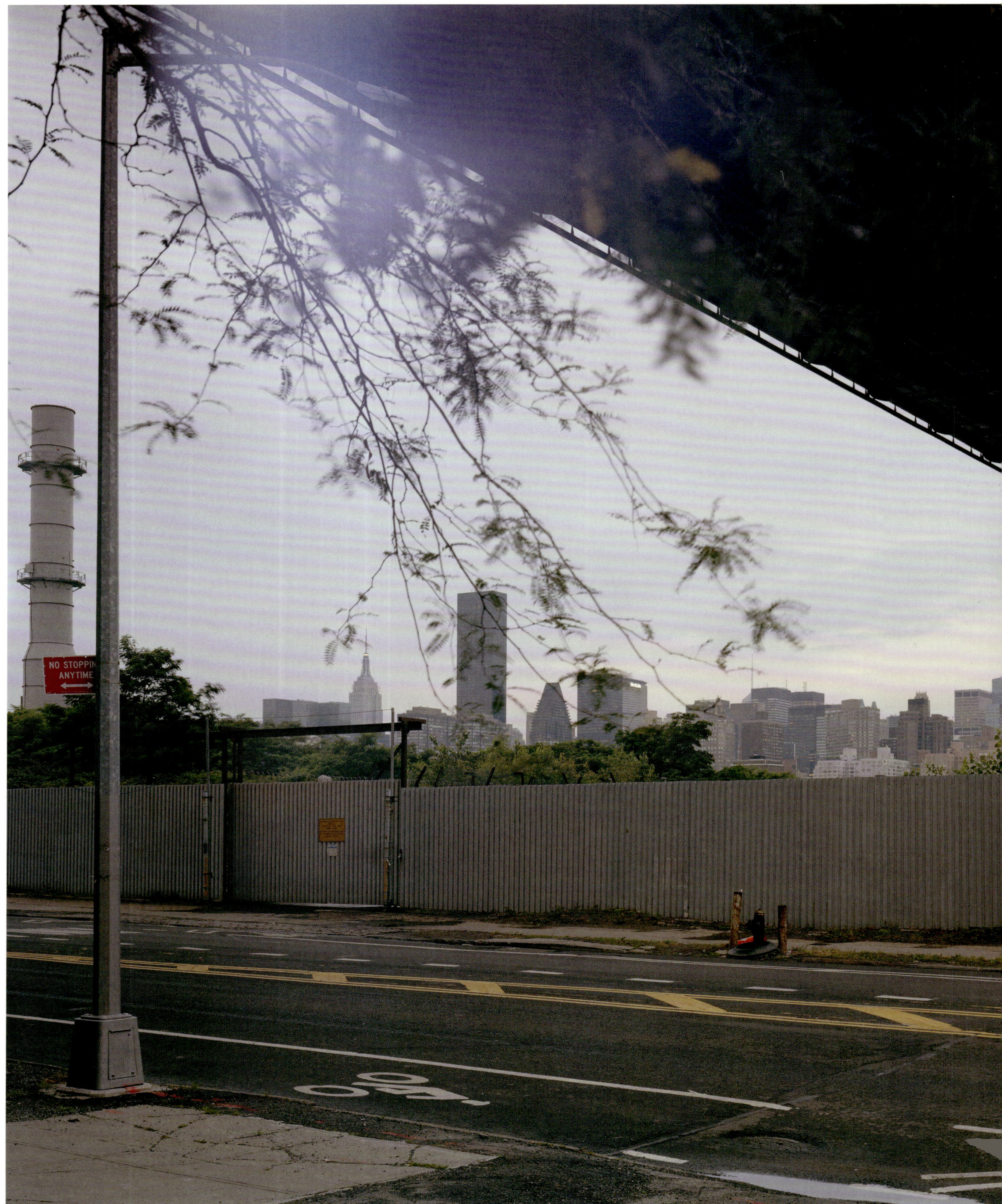

NO STOPPING
ANYTIME

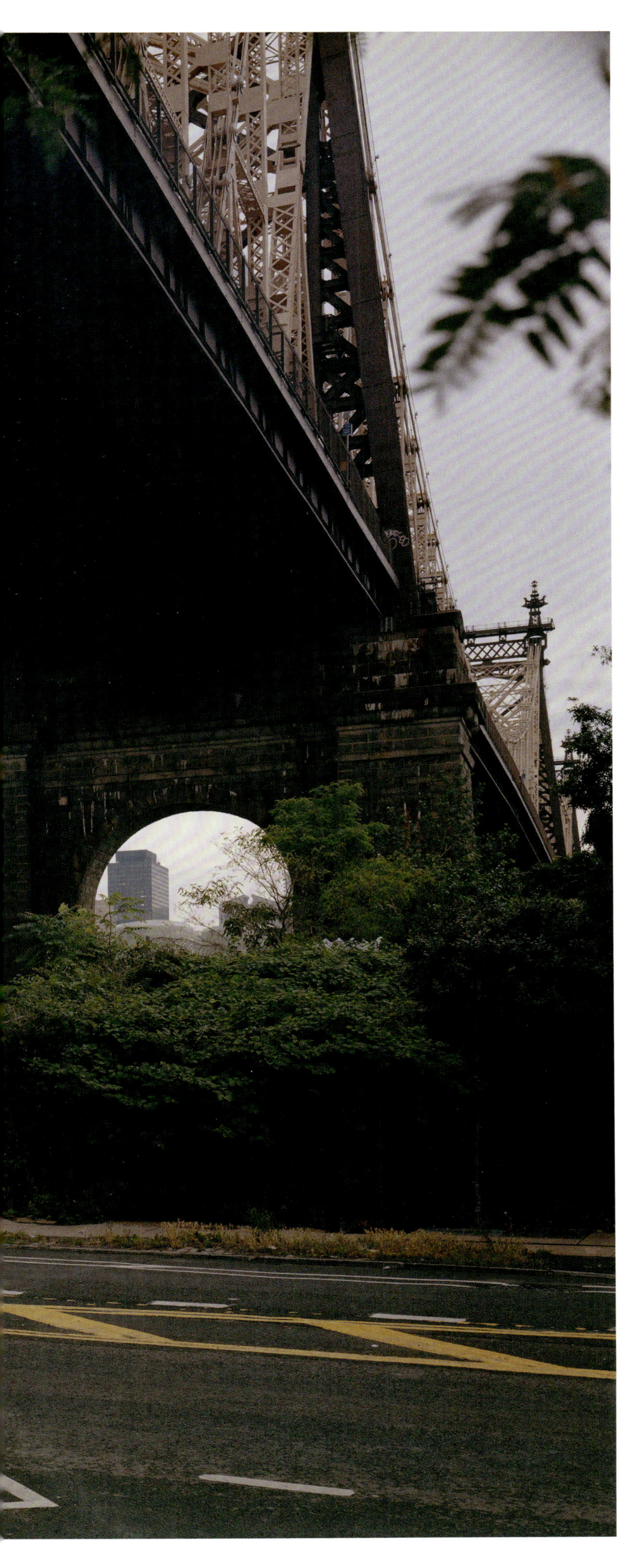

Paul Simon was coming home at around 6 in the morning walking along the Queensboro Bridge over the East River when he got an idea for a song.
That song became "59th Street Bridge Song (Feelin' Groovy)."

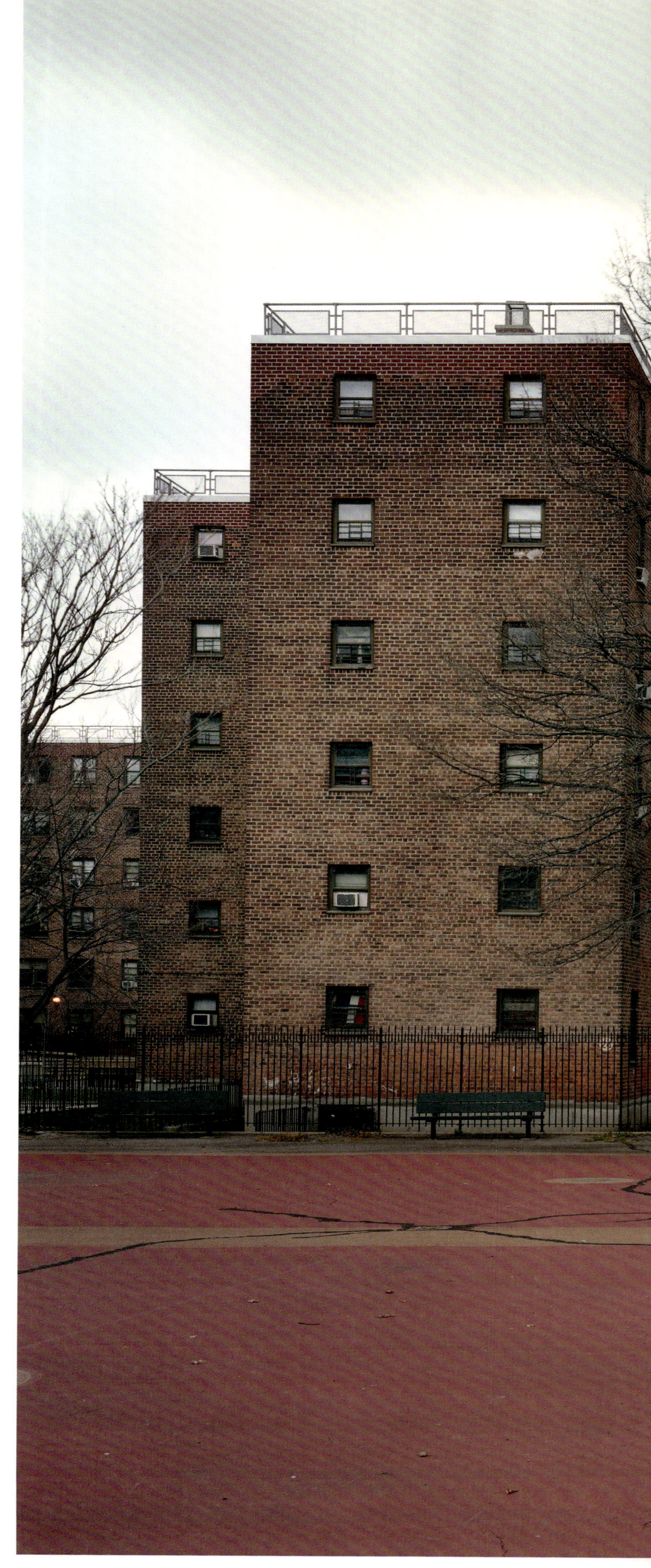

Marcy Houses is a public housing complex
in Bedford-Stuyvesant, Brooklyn, with twenty-seven
six-story buildings containing 1,705 apartments.
In 1981, in one of these buildings, twelve-year-old
Shawn Corey Carter pulled a gun on his drug-addicted
brother Eric and shot him in the shoulder after
he discovered he had stolen his rings.
In the neighborhood, Shawn is known by
his nickname, Jay-Z.

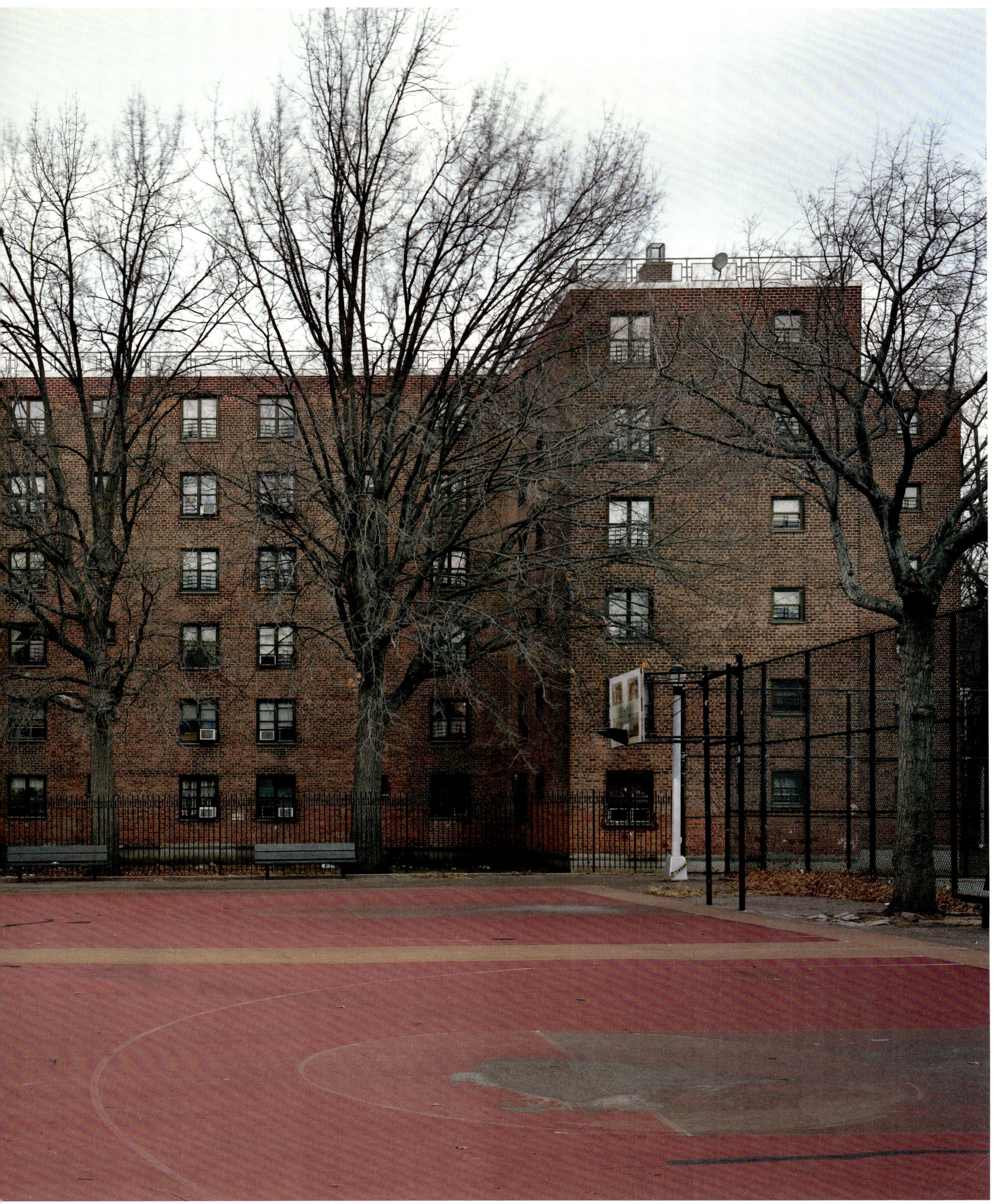

The Pythian Temple located at 135 West 70th Street
was built to serve as a clubhouse for the Order of the
Knights of Pythias, a fraternal organization founded
in Washington during the Civil War.
In the 1940s, the Pythians leased a space in the building
to Decca Records, who created an acoustically renowned
music recording studio in it.
In 1954, Bill Haley & His Comets recorded their
hit song "Rock Around The Clock" here.
The Pythian Temple was converted into luxury
condominiums in 1982.

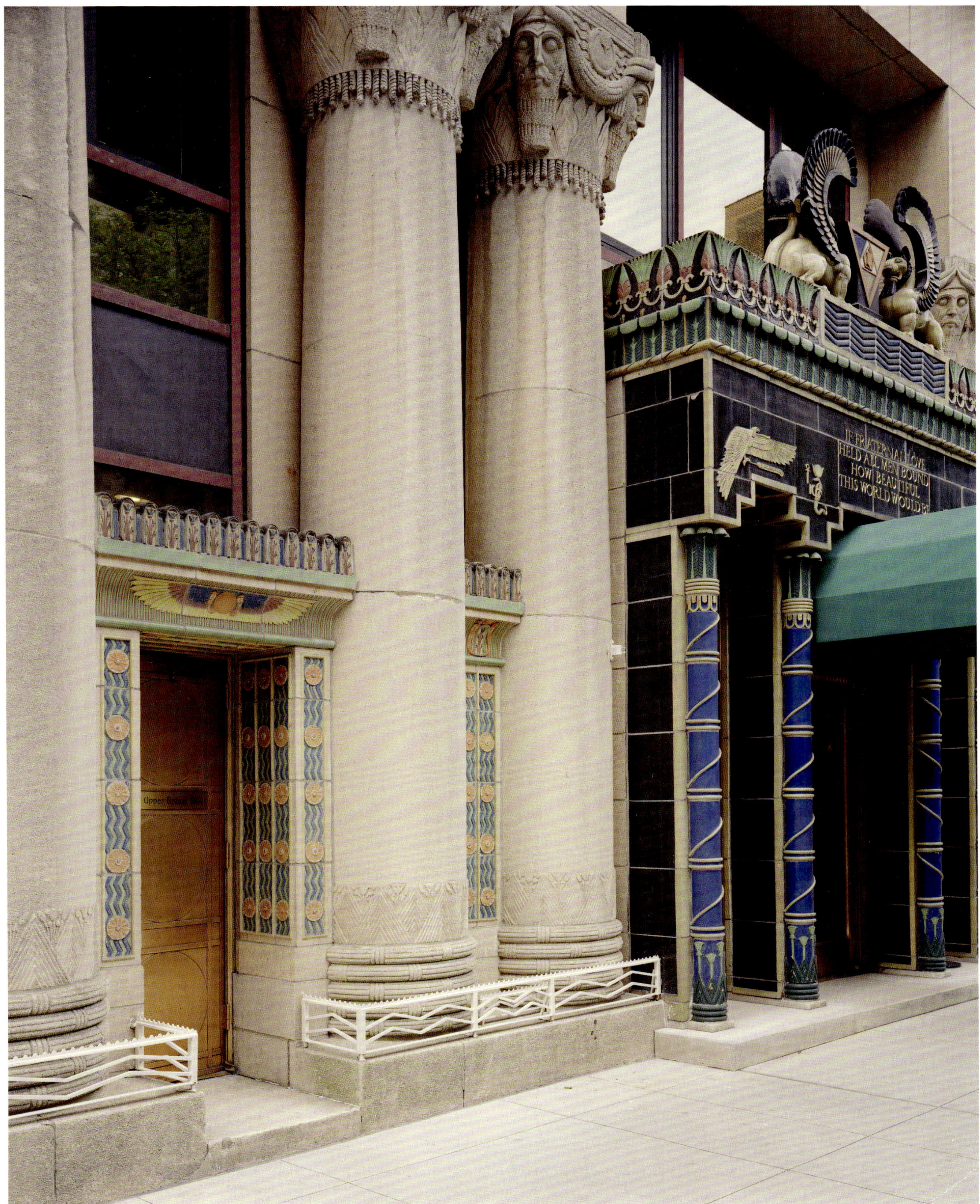

IF FRATERNAL LOVE
HELD ALL MEN BOUND
HOW BEAUTIFUL
THIS WORLD WOULD BE
Upper Bazar St

Max's Kansas City was a nightclub and restaurant
at 213 Park Avenue South. It opened in 1965 and closed
in November 1981.
According to one of the regulars, Andy Warhol, it was
the place where pop art and pop life came together.
One late night in 1971, Iggy Pop was staying nearby
in the apartment of his friend, Danny Fields, watching
a movie on TV. Danny called and told him to come down
to Max's Kansas City because there was someone
he should definitely meet.
Iggy entered the club, headed towards the bar, and was
introduced to David Bowie.

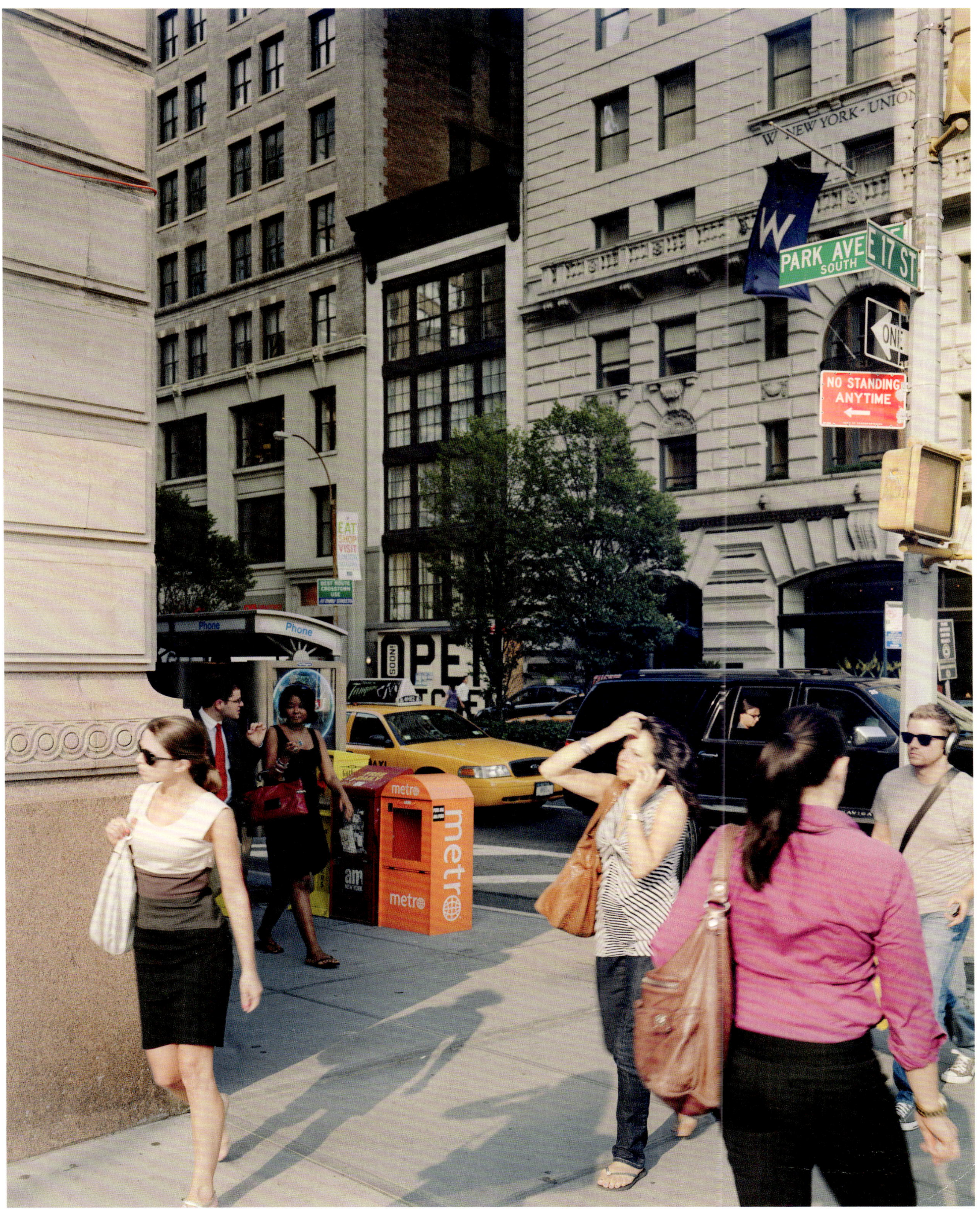
W NEW YORK - UNION
W
PARK AVE SOUTH
E 17 ST
ONE
NO STANDING ANYTIME
Phone
Phone
metro
metro
metro
am NEW YORK
EAT SHOP VISIT
OPEN

In 1979, the movie *The Warriors* by Walter Hill told
the story of a street gang from Coney Island, Brooklyn,
fighting all night against every other gang in New York
to make its way back home from the Bronx.
At that time Coney Island was the turf of a real street gang
called The Homicides Inc.
The entire film was shot at night on the streets of New York.
The only daytime scene is the last one, in which
The Warriors finally return to Coney Island after a night
of battle. As the gang members walk on the beach
and the closing titles run on the screen a song is playing.
It's "In The City" by Joe Walsh.

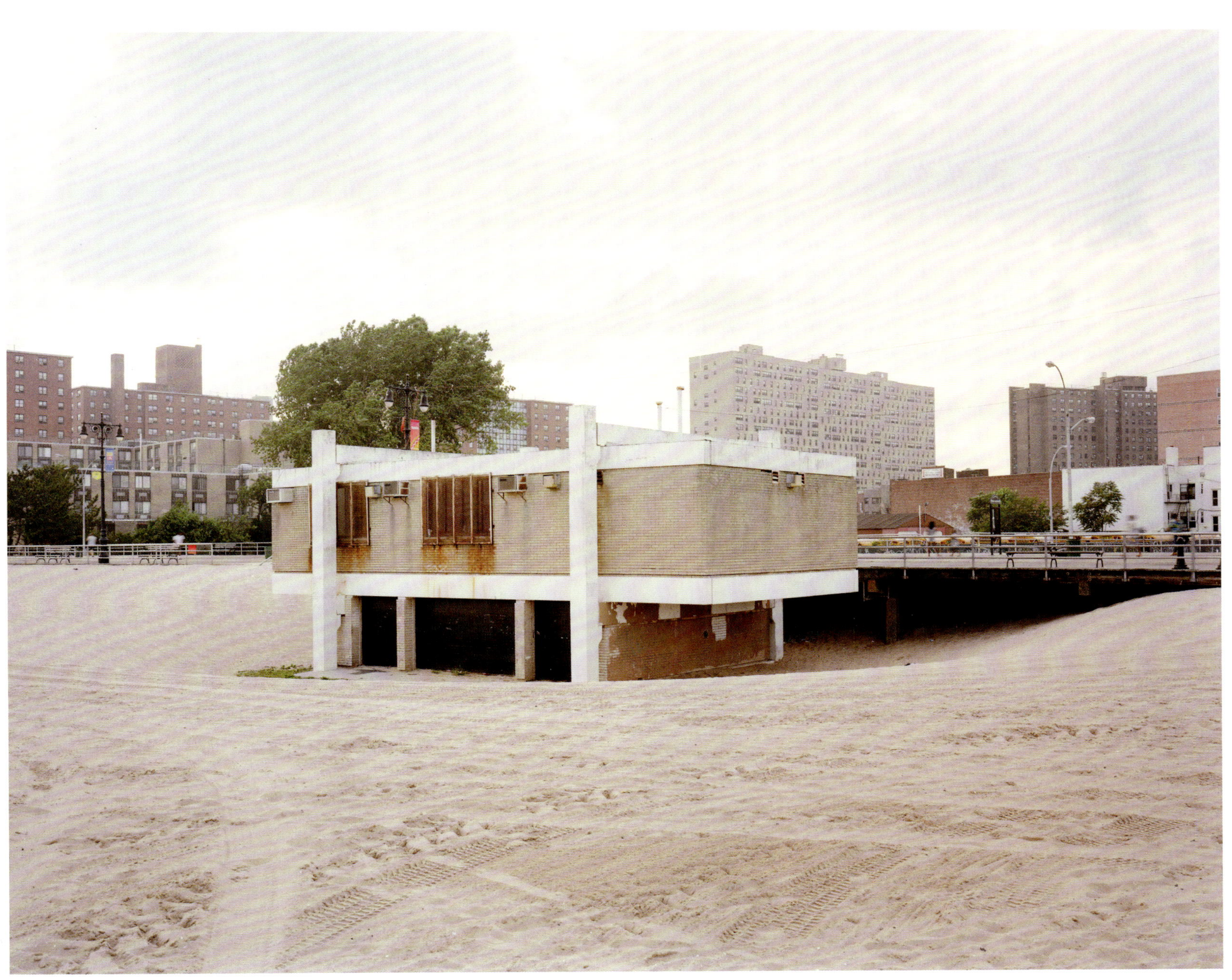

Jeffrey Ross Hyman was born in Forest Hills, Queens.
He said he spent most of his teenage years sitting
on the corner off Queens Boulevard drinking and insulting
people and hanging out at the rock club The Coventry.
His mother Charlotte had kicked him out of the family home
and he had moved into her art gallery with a sleeping bag,
a pillow, and a blanket.
One night at The Coventry he met Douglas Colvin and
brought him to the art gallery to sleep on the floor.
Douglas introduced him to John Cummings, a friend that
had just bought a blue Mosrite Ventures II guitar for 54 dollars.
They formed a band, changed their names to Joey,
Dee Dee, and Johnny Ramone, and crafted the sound and
aesthetics of punk rock with their band, The Ramones.

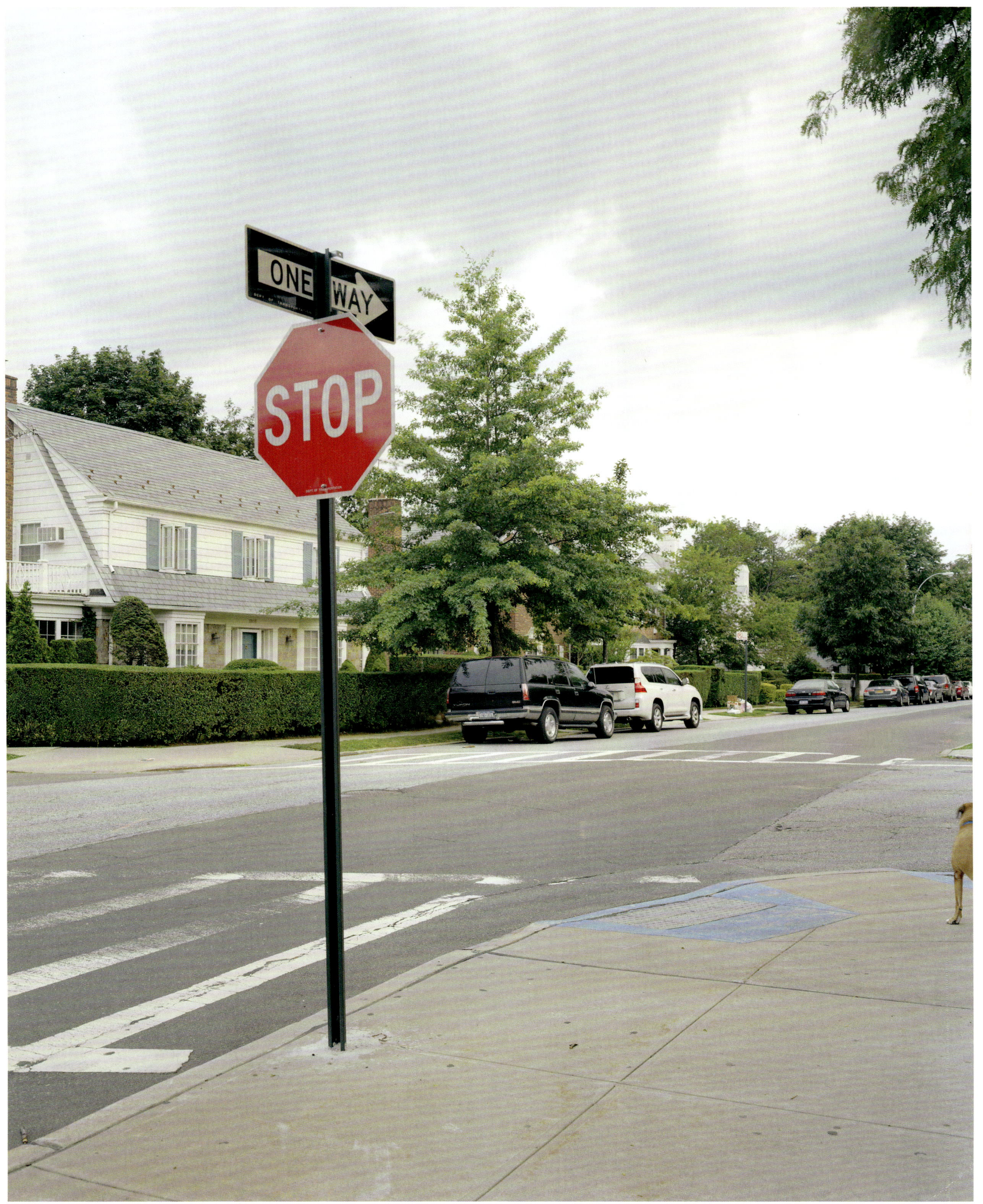

ONE WAY
STOP

In 1972, Bobby Womack wrote and performed
the theme song of the blaxploitation movie
Across 110th Street.
110th Street is commonly known as the boundary
between Central Park and Harlem.
In the lyrics, Womack describes Harlem as:
"The capital of every ghetto town"

(*Across 110th Street*. Writer/s: Womack, Bobby. Publisher:
Sony/ATV Music Publishing LLC).

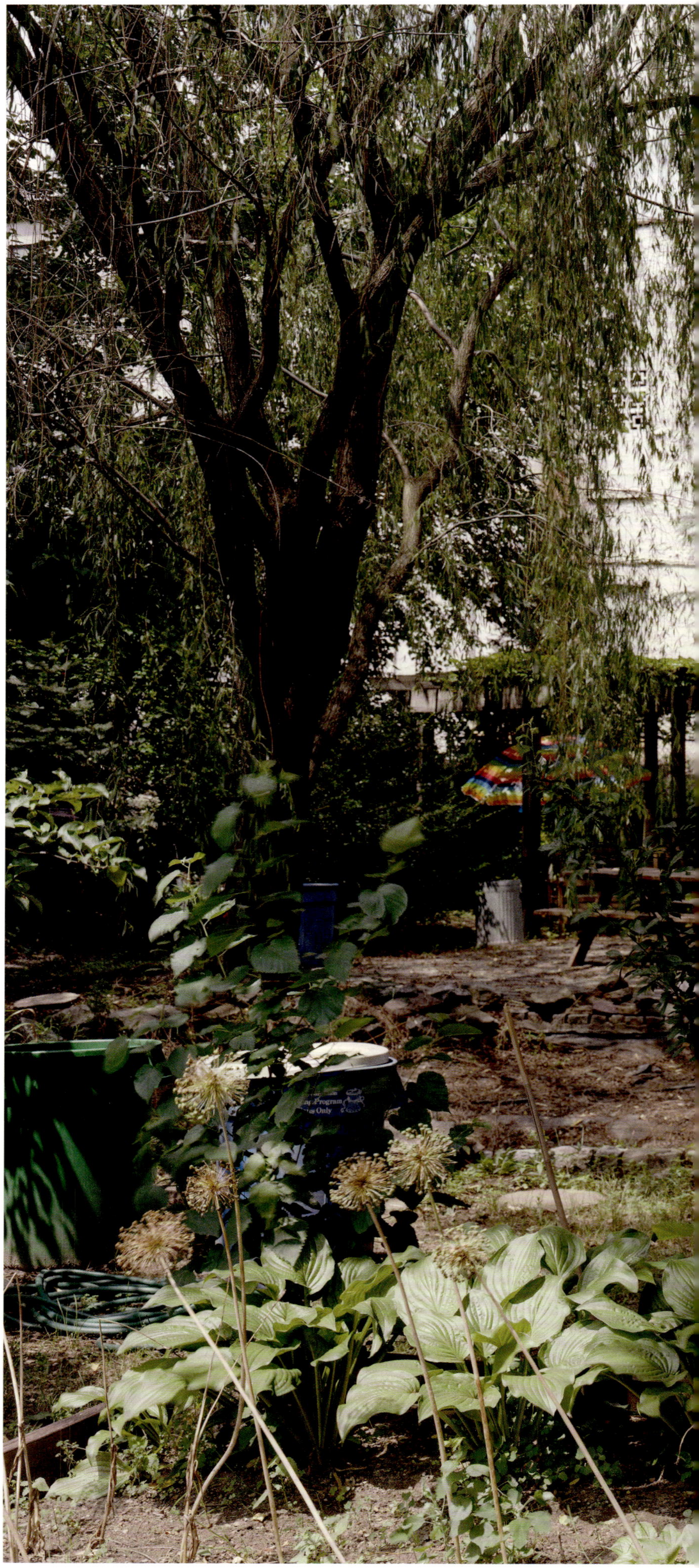

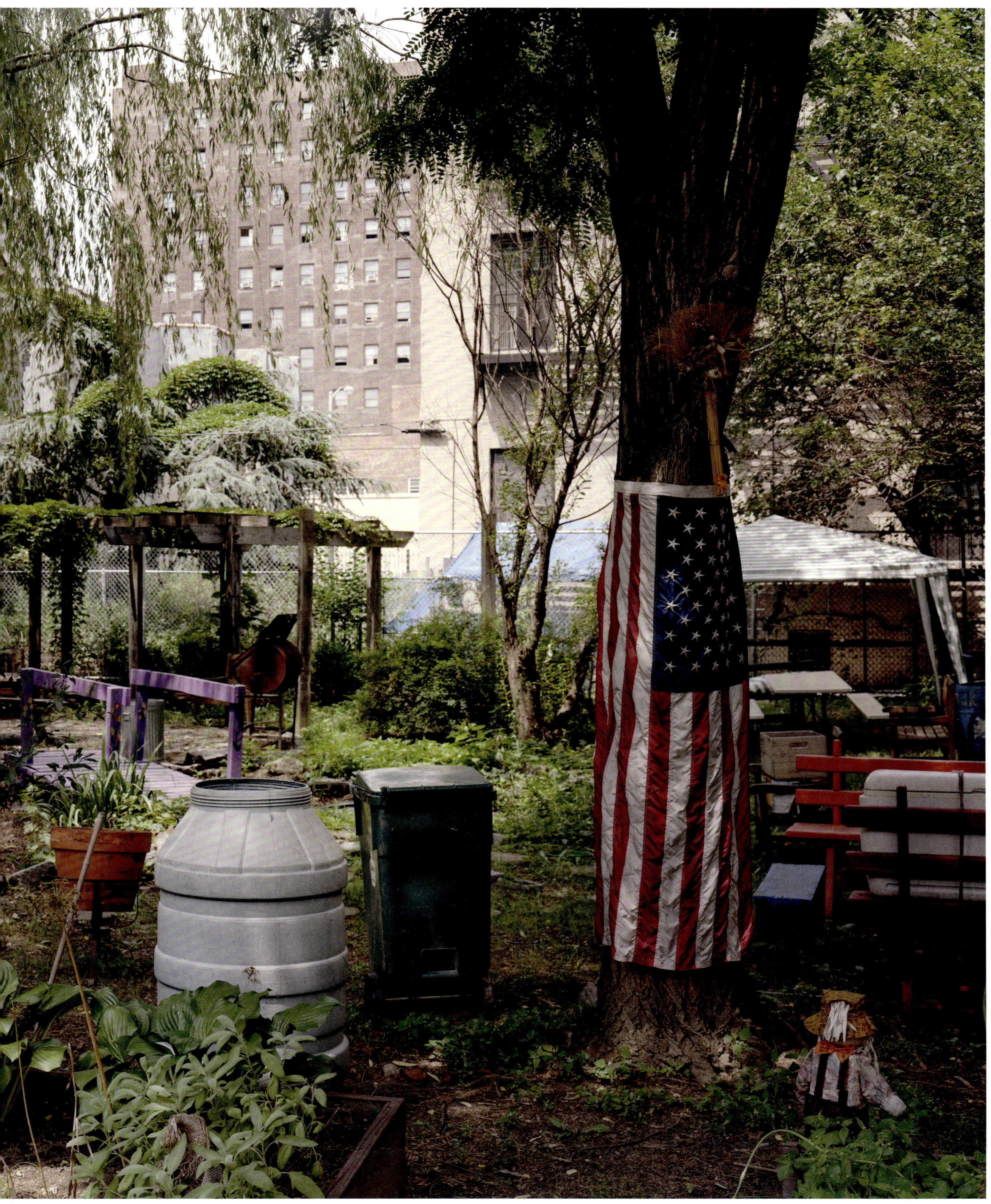

The Folklore Center at 110 MacDougal Street was
a small shop owned by Izzy Young that sold and reported
on everything that had to do with folk music.
In the early 1960s, it was the meeting point of the
"Americana" folk scene.
Bob Dylan spent most of his early days in New York here.

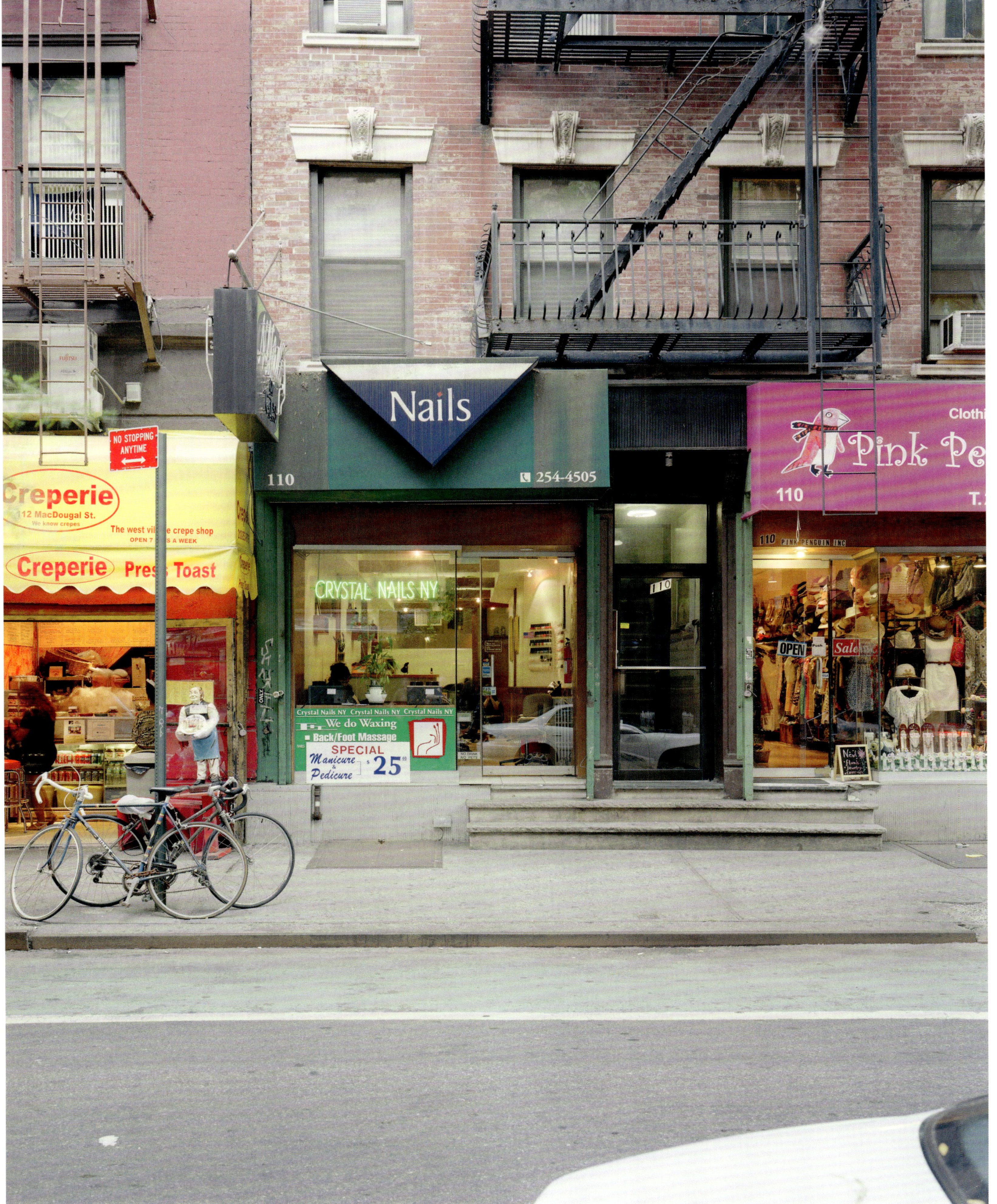
Nails
110
254-4505
Creperie
112 MacDougal St.
We know crepes
The west village crepe shop
OPEN 7 DAYS A WEEK
Creperie   Press Toast
NO STOPPING ANYTIME
CRYSTAL NAILS NY
Crystal Nails NY Crystal Nails NY Crystal Nails NY
We do Waxing
Back/Foot Massage
SPECIAL
Manicure
Pedicure $25
Clothi
Pink Pe
110
110 PINK PENGUIN INC
OPEN
Sale

In 2010, after sixteen years of legal troubles and drug
problems, soul singer, poet, social activist, and godfather
of rap Gil Scott-Heron released his thirteenth and final album,
"I'm New Here," in which he deals with themes of regret,
reconciliation, and redemption.
One of the songs is titled "New York Is Killing Me."
Gil Scott-Heron passed away on May 27, 2011 at St. Luke's
Hospital in New York.

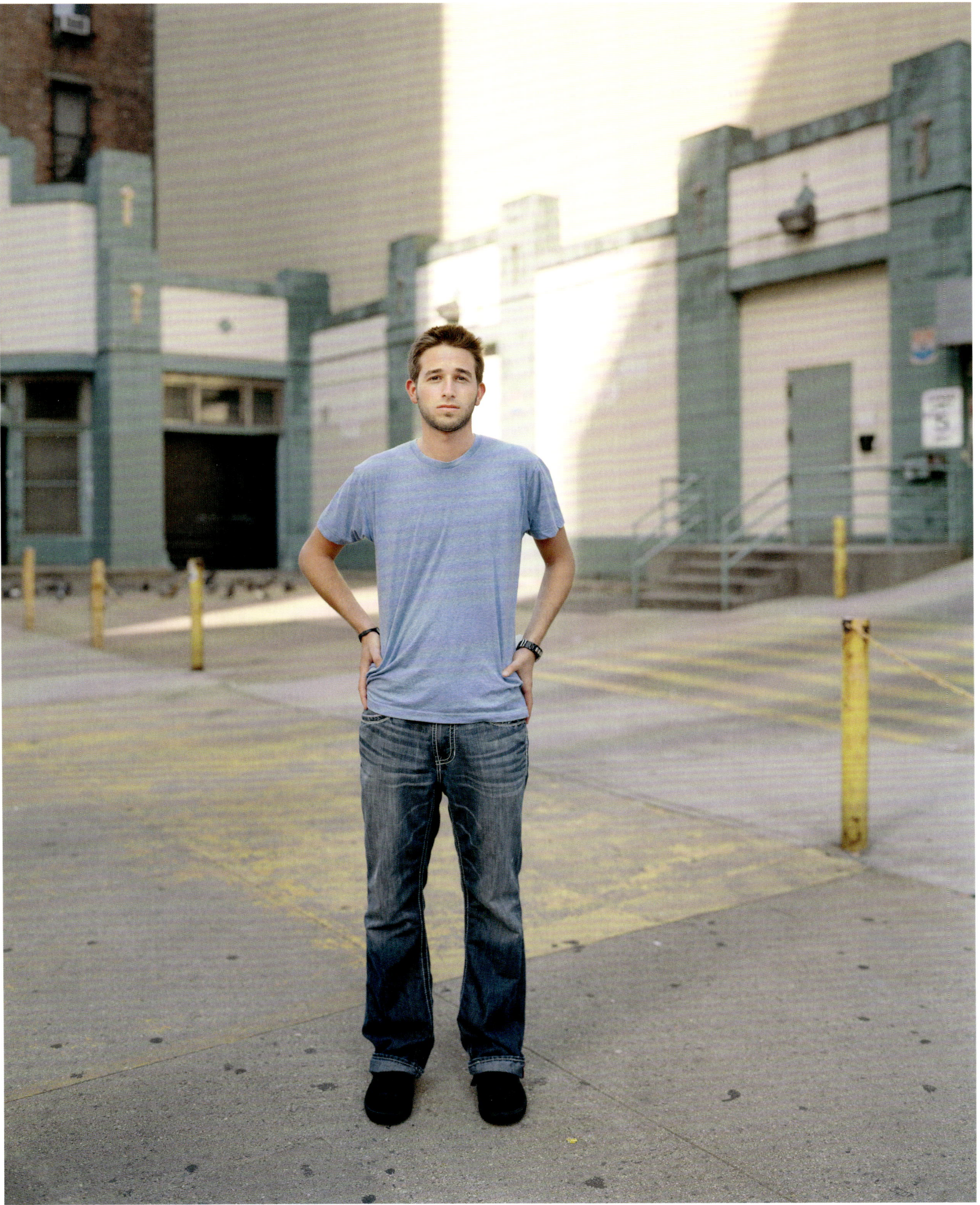

Popeye's Spinach Factory was a club at 2301 Emmons
Avenue in Sheepshead Bay, Brooklyn, that offered live music
seven days a week mostly for a crowd of drunken people.
On March 29, 1974 punk band The Dictators were playing
their usual set of songs when their roadie, Richard Blum,
jumped on stage to deliver a terrific performance
of "Wild Things." The audience went crazy.
Richard had never set foot on a stage before, except
for fixing equipment. That night he became the frontman
and "secret weapon" of the band and changed his name
to "Handsome Dick" Manitoba.

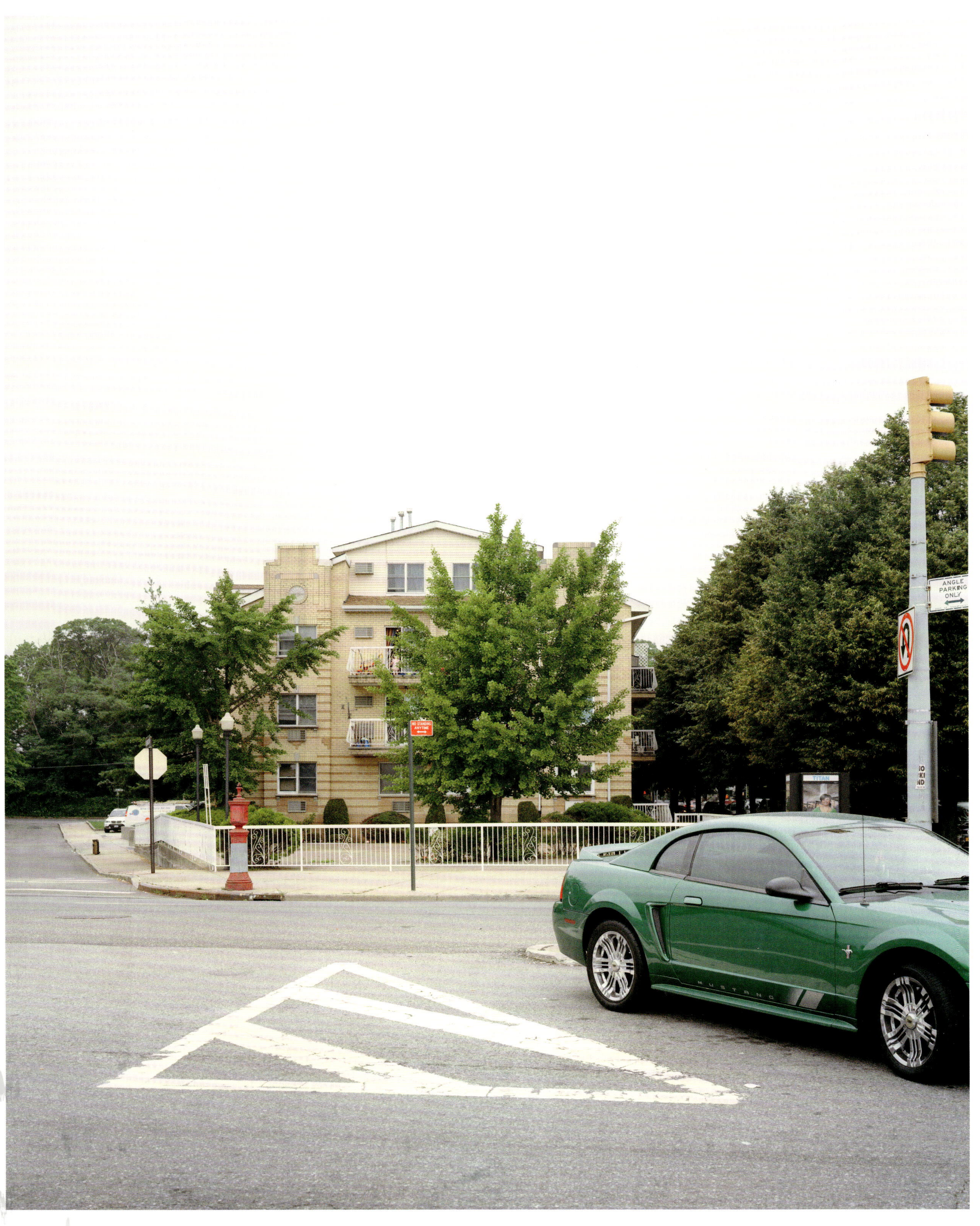

ANGLE
PARKING
ONLY
NO STANDING
ANYTIME
TITAN
MUSTANG

Director Michel Gondry used thirty-two identical Ludwig
drum kits and sixteen identical microphone stands
to shoot the videoclip for "The Hardest Button To Button"
by The White Stripes.
The video was filmed around Riverside Drive in Harlem.
The drum kits were donated to a local music school
after shooting.

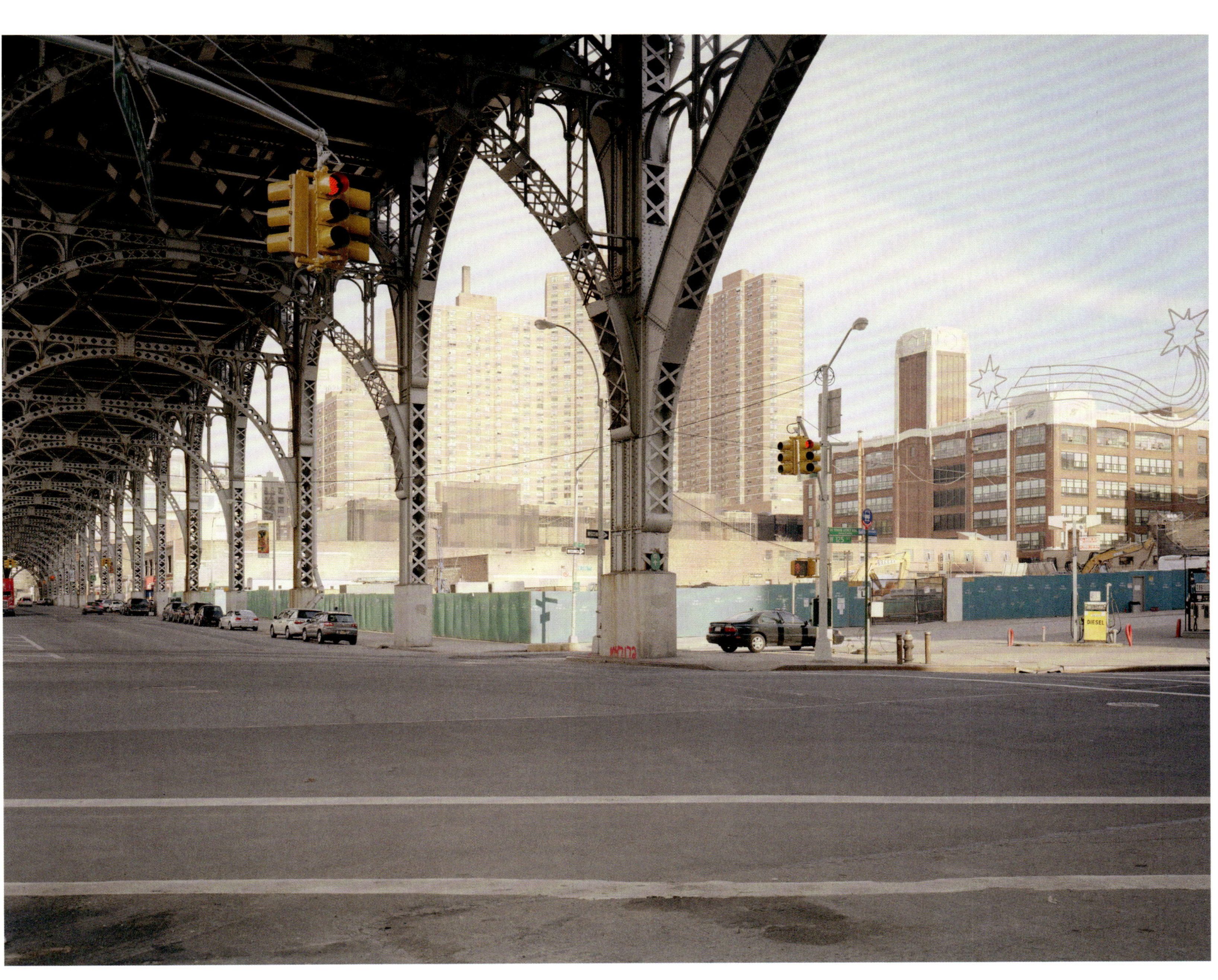

On October 16, 1971 John Lennon and Yoko Ono
moved to their first New York apartment
at 105 Bank Street in Greenwich Village, renting
it from Joe Butler of The Lovin' Spoonful.
It had two large rooms and a wrought-iron staircase
that led up to a small roof garden.

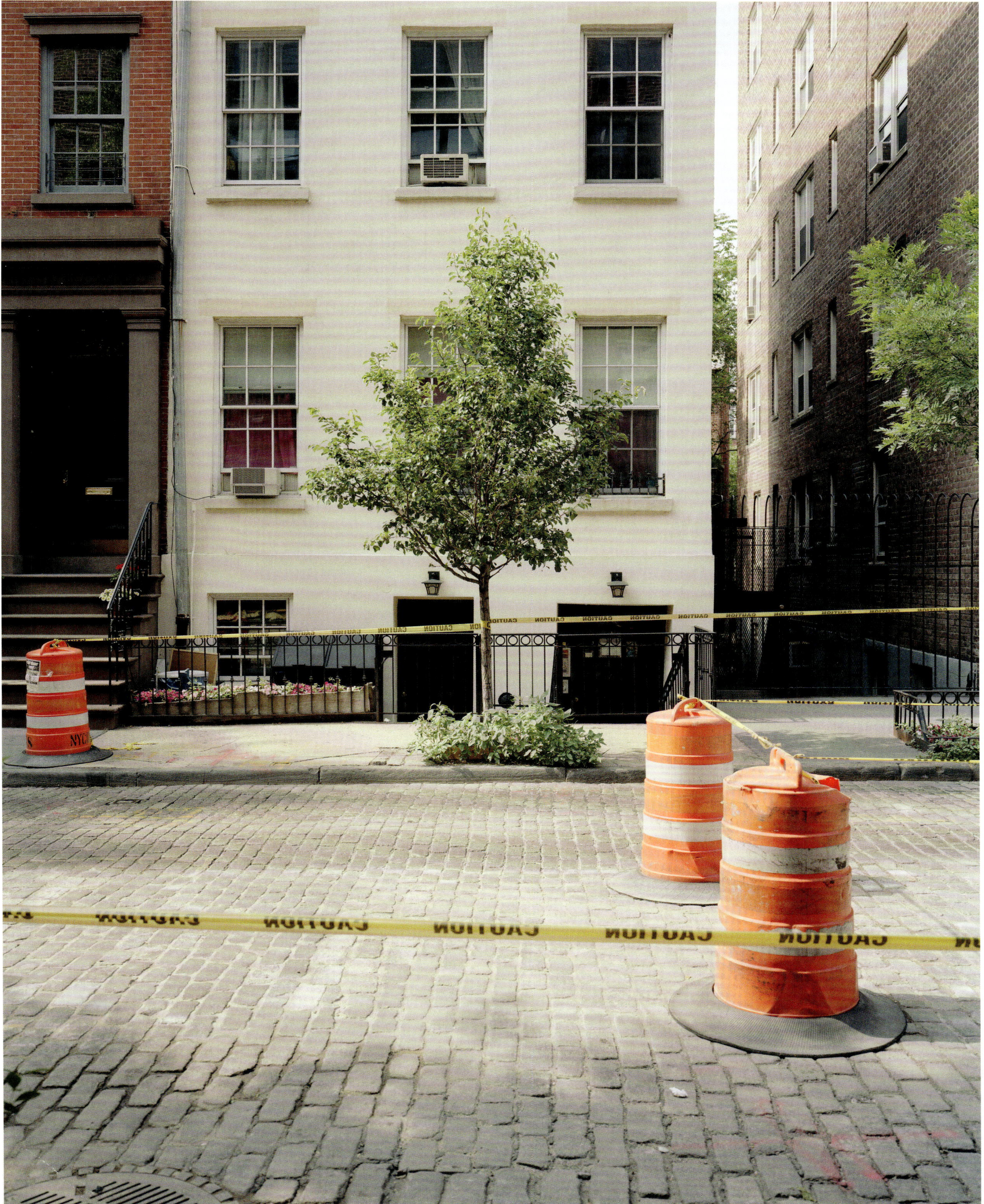

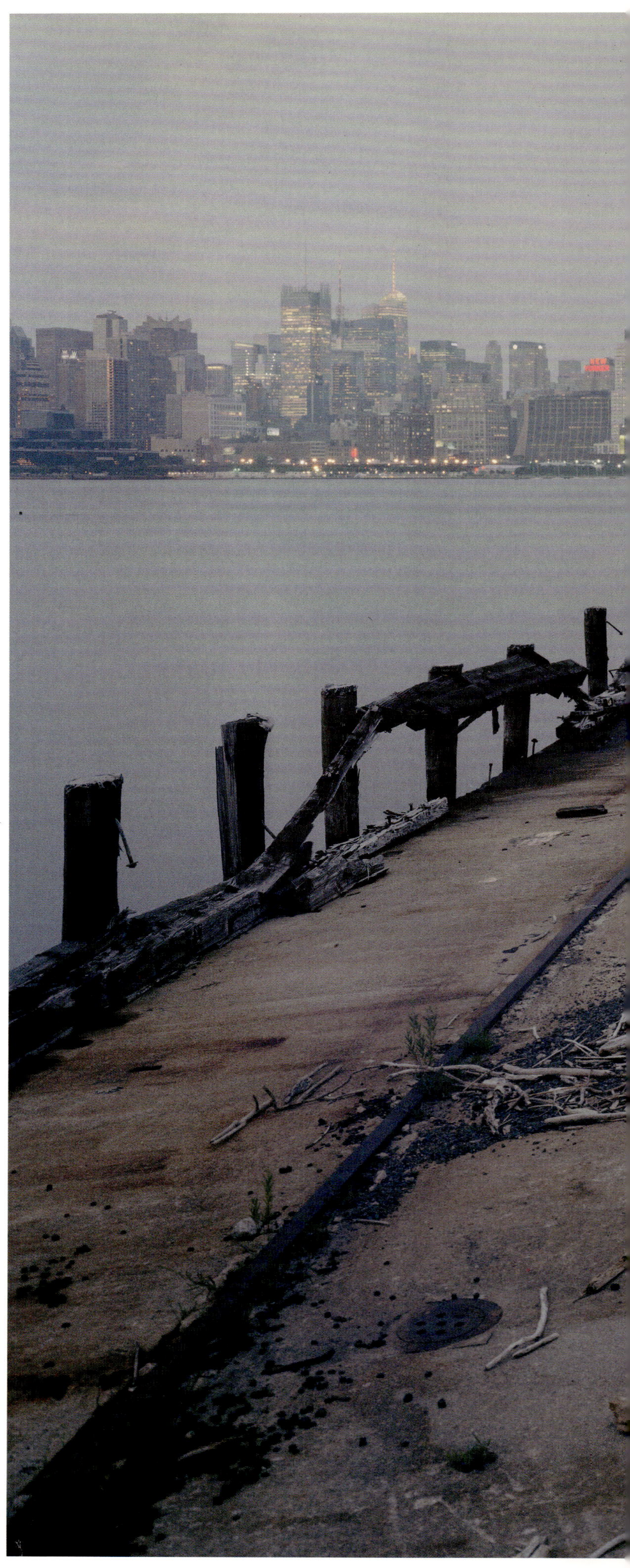

Hoboken, New Jersey, is the birthplace of baseball
and Frank Sinatra. It's also home to Maxwell's,
a club opened in 1978 by Steve Fallon that became
a vital part of the independent rock community during
the 1980s and early 1990s.
Hoboken's indie rock band Yo La Tengo used
to rent Maxwell's every year during Hanukkah and play
eight consecutive nights accompanied by many
comedians and musicians.
In 2000, they closed their ninth album with
"Night Falls On Hoboken," a 17-minute epic track
dedicated to their hometown.

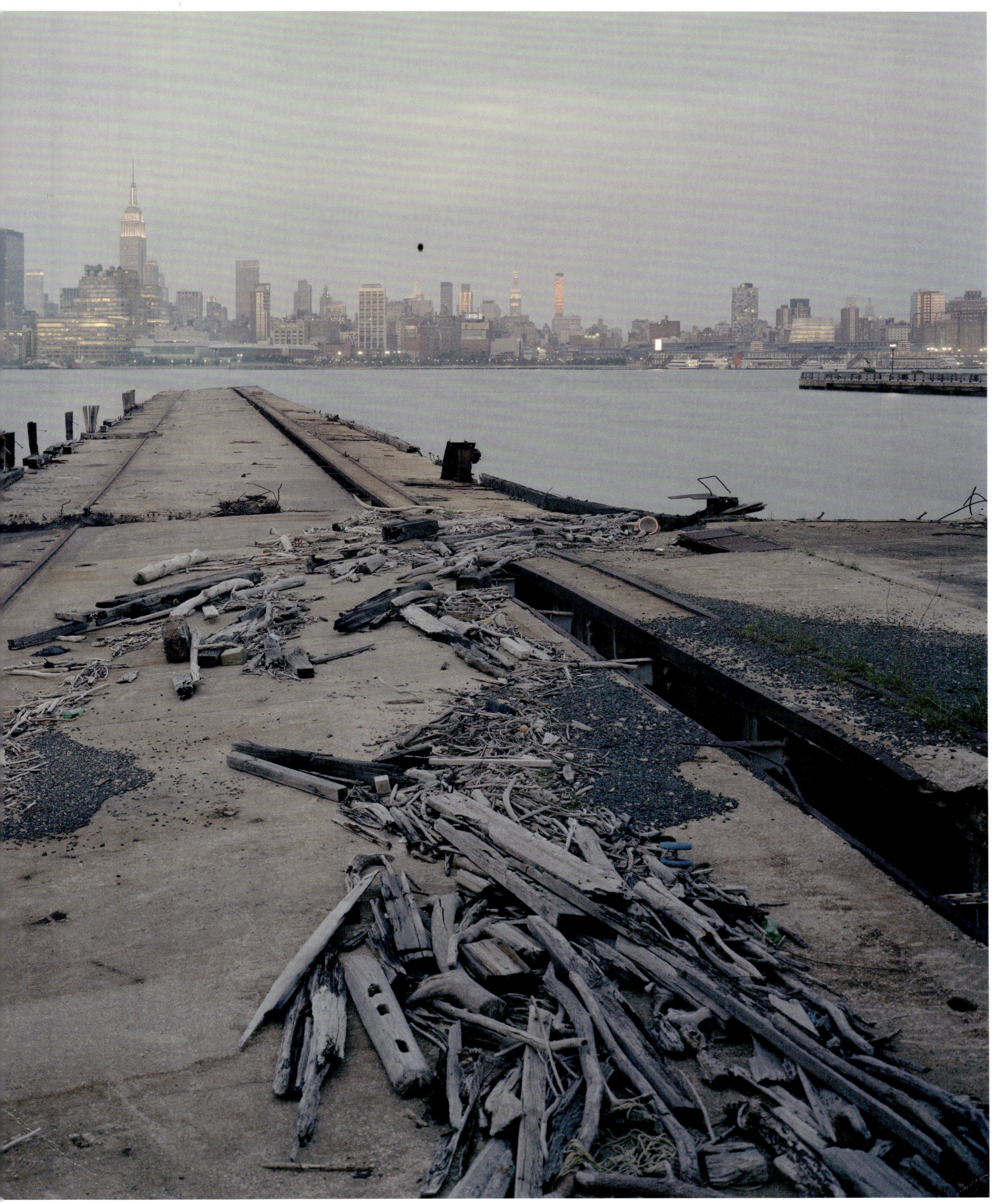

The Brill Building at 1619 Broadway was named
after the Brill Brothers, whose clothing store was first
located on the corner.
After its completion in 1931, the owners were forced
to rent space to music publishers. By 1962 the Brill
Building hosted 165 music companies. Musicians could
write a song then go to another floor and book an hour
at a studio, hire some of the musicians that hung around,
cut a demo, and take the song around the building
to record companies, publishers, and managers.
The Brill Building was the doorway to stardom for every
artist on the New York music scene.

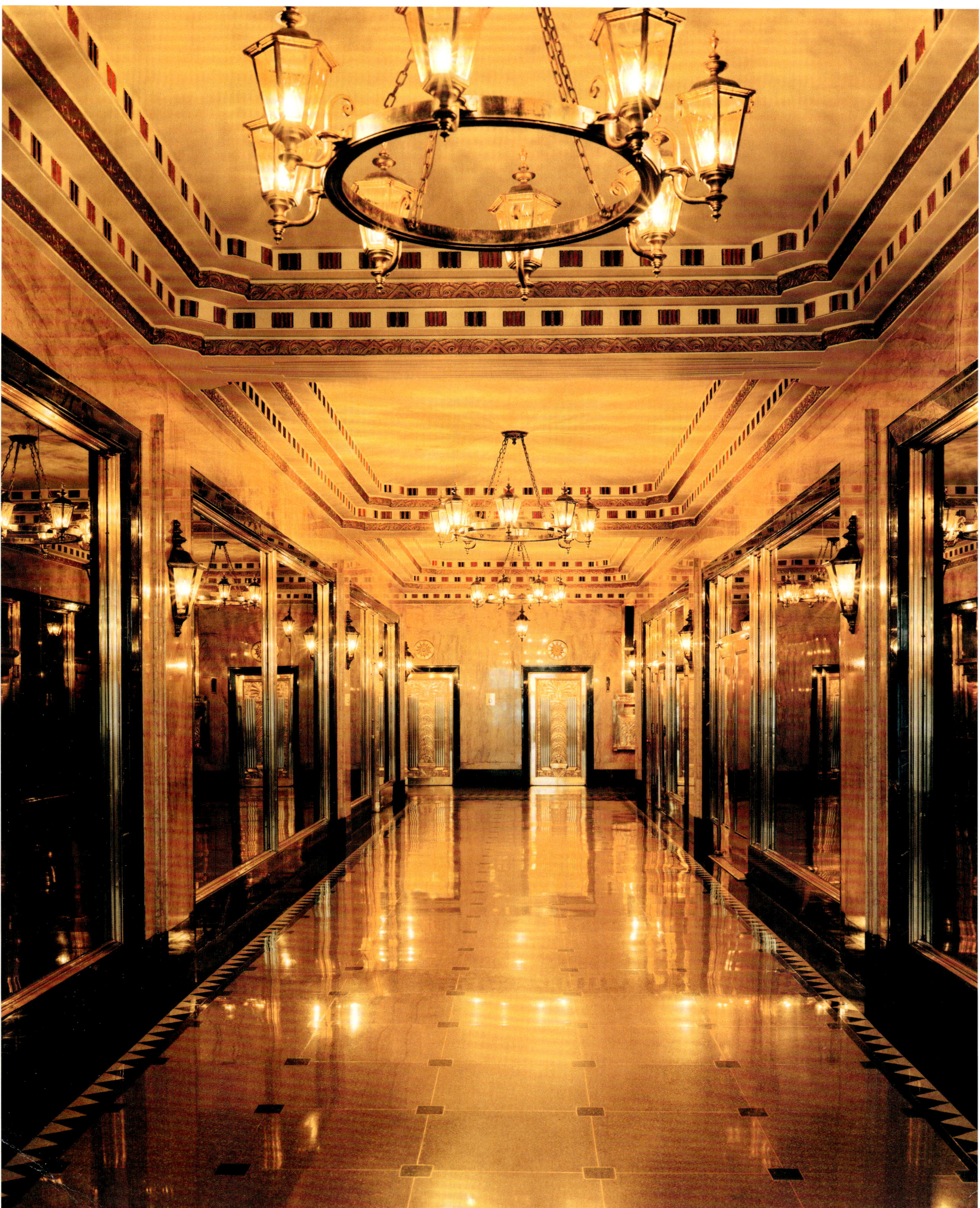

The corner between 53rd and 3rd in Manhattan
was a well-known spot for male prostitution in New York,
known as "The Loop."
The Ramones named their second single after it.
The song, written by Dee Dee Ramone, tells the story
of a man who prostitutes himself at the corner.
He is finally picked up but kills his customer with a razor blade.

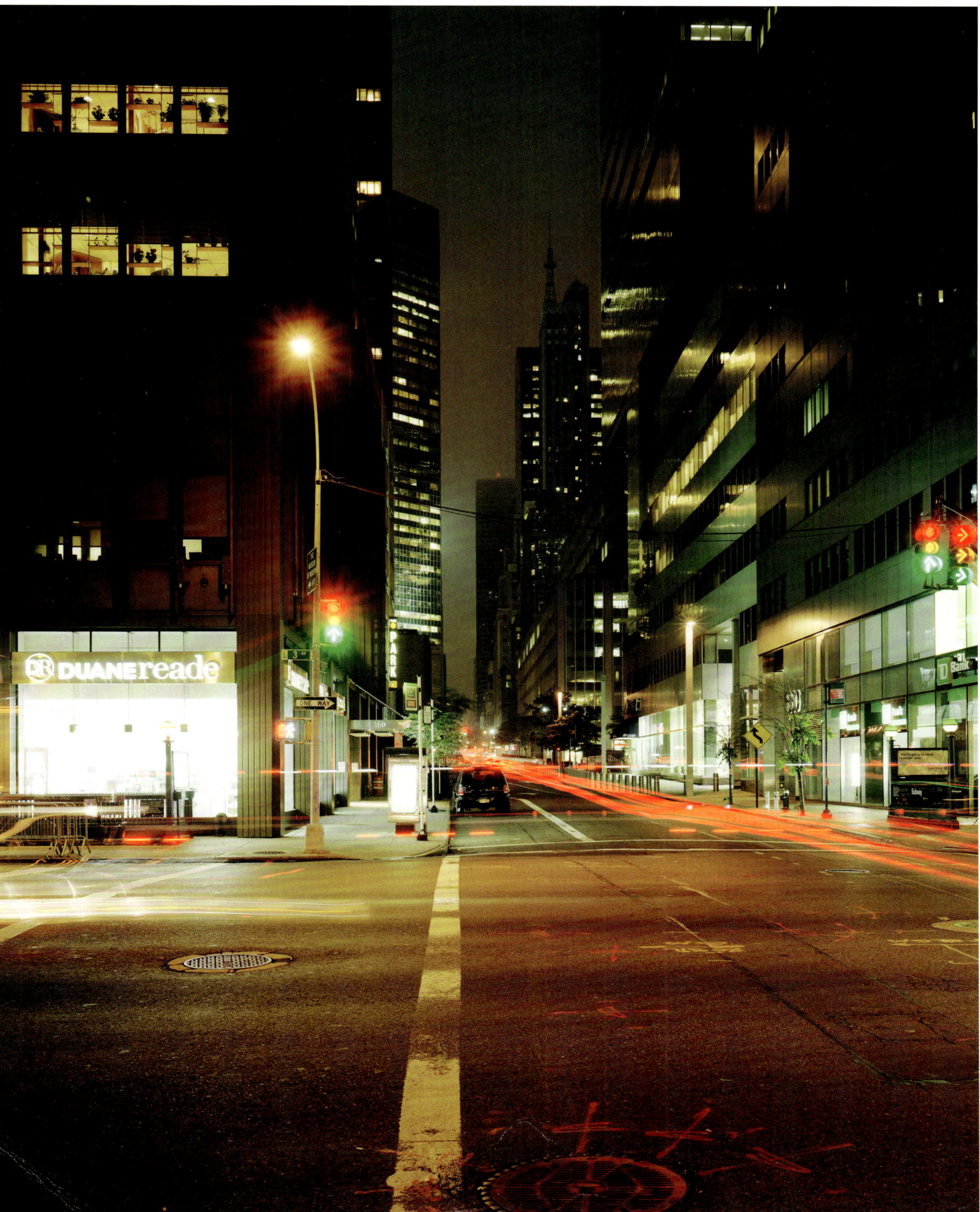

In the early 1960s, Woody Guthrie had been confined
to a mental hospital in New Jersey. Bob Dylan often
went to visit him.
One day Woody told him he had a box of lyrics and poems
stored in the basement of his house on Mermaid Avenue,
Coney Island, and that he was free to turn them into songs.
Bob Dylan went all the way to 3520 Mermaid Avenue,
but felt uncomfortable searching through Woody's house
in his absence. So he left without the songs.
Nearly forty years later, Woody's daughter, Nora Guthrie,
discovered the box of lyrics and poems and gave them
to Billy Bragg and the band Wilco.
They recorded and released them in 1998 on the album
"Mermaid Avenue."

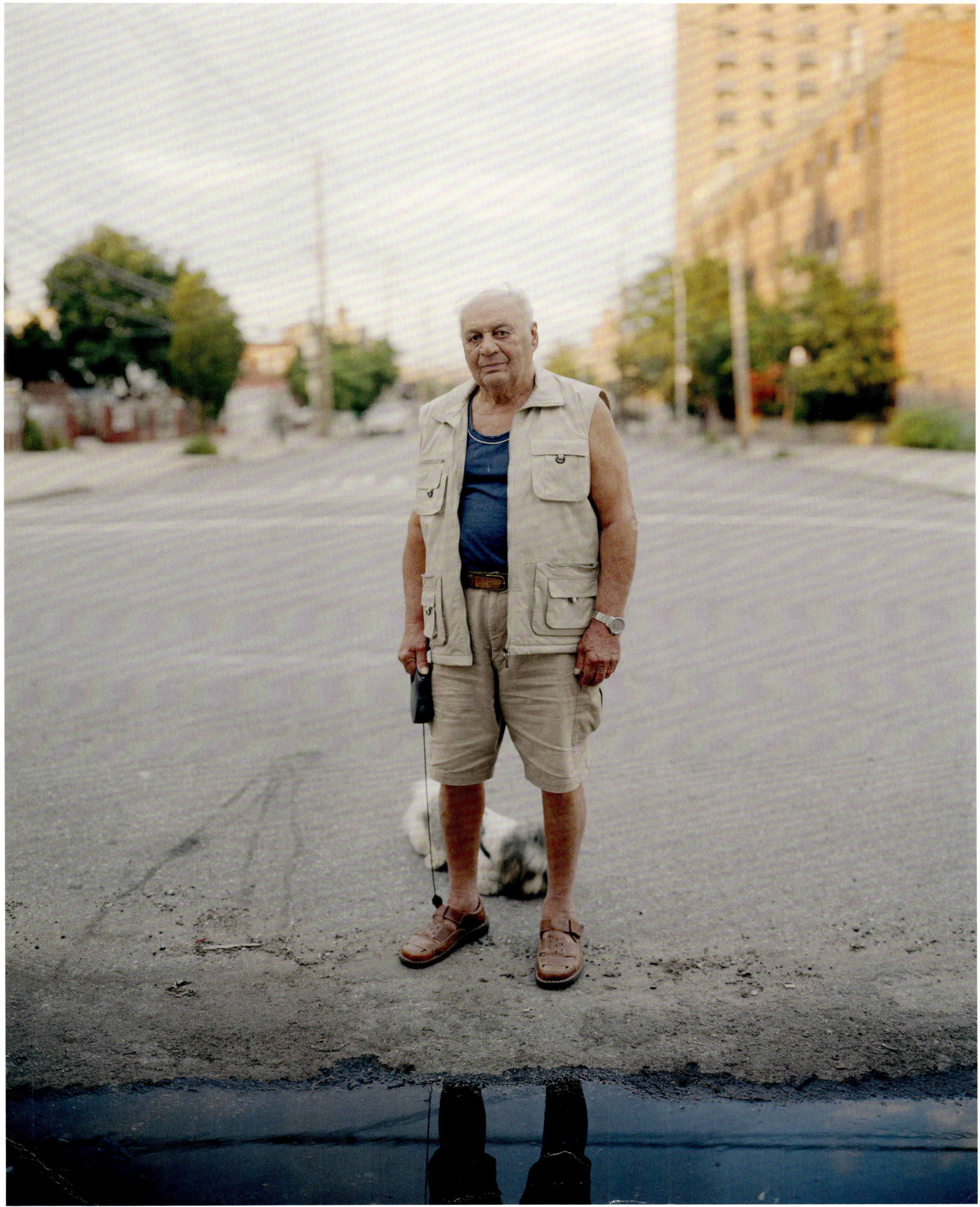

Debbie Harry's first apartment in New York was only one
block away from CBGB on the Bowery. The ground floor
had been turned into an illegal liquor store and there was
no heating in the building.
Debbie described the apartment as a "Bowery hellhole"
and said she was sure it was haunted by a poltergeist.

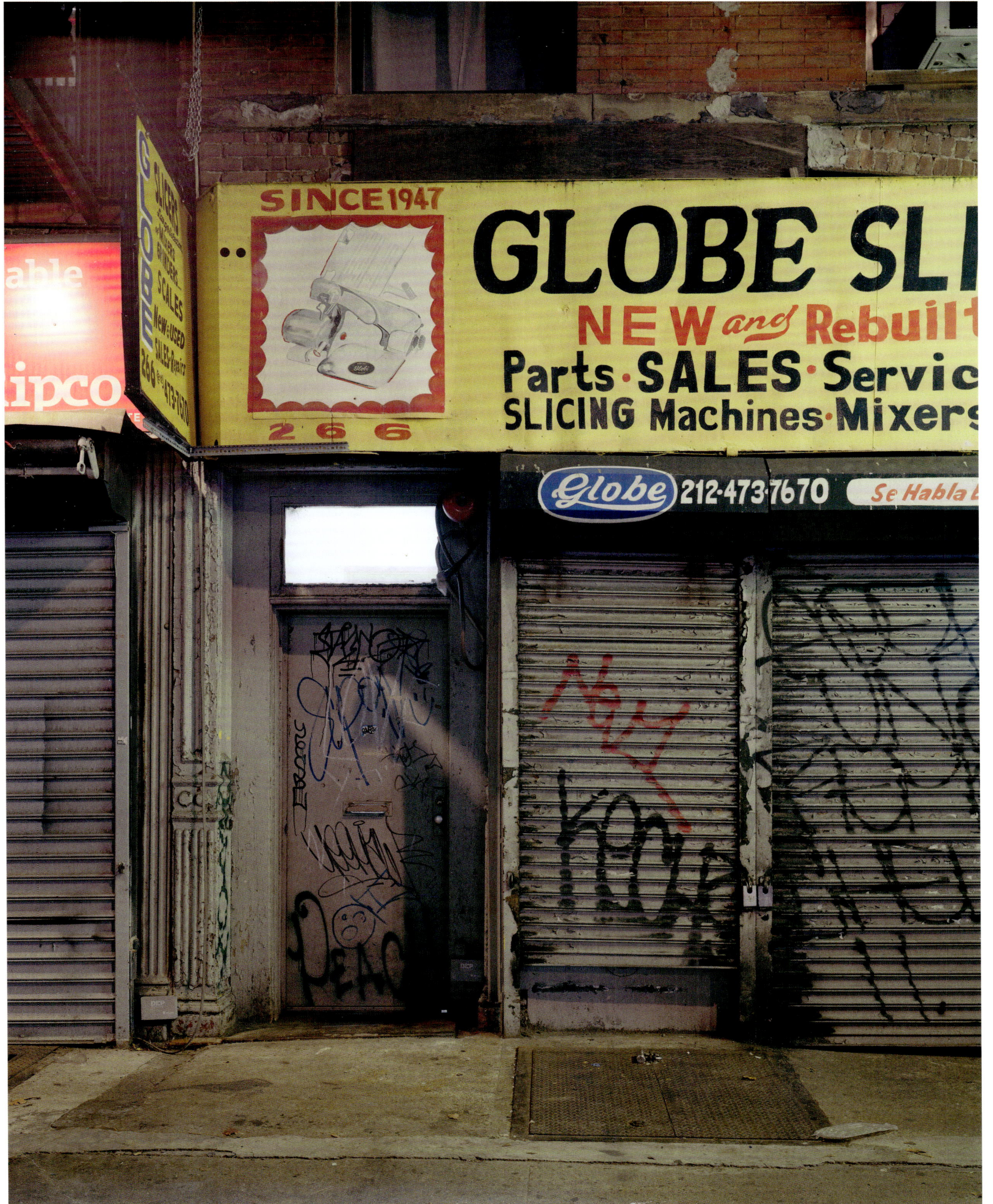
SINCE 1947
266
GLOBE SLI
NEW and Rebuilt
Parts · SALES · Servic
SLICING Machines · Mixers
Globe 212·473·7670 Se Habla
SLICERS
GRINDERS
SCALES
New & USED
SALES Repair
266
473-7670
able
ipco

Lou Reed and John Cale spoke to one another, after
a long time of silence, at Andy Warhol's memorial service
in New York on April 1, 1987.
Painter Julian Schnabel suggested they write a memorial
piece for Warhol. On January 7, 1989 Lou Reed and John
Cale performed the album "Songs For Drella" dedicated
to Warhol at the Church of St. Ann's in Brooklyn.

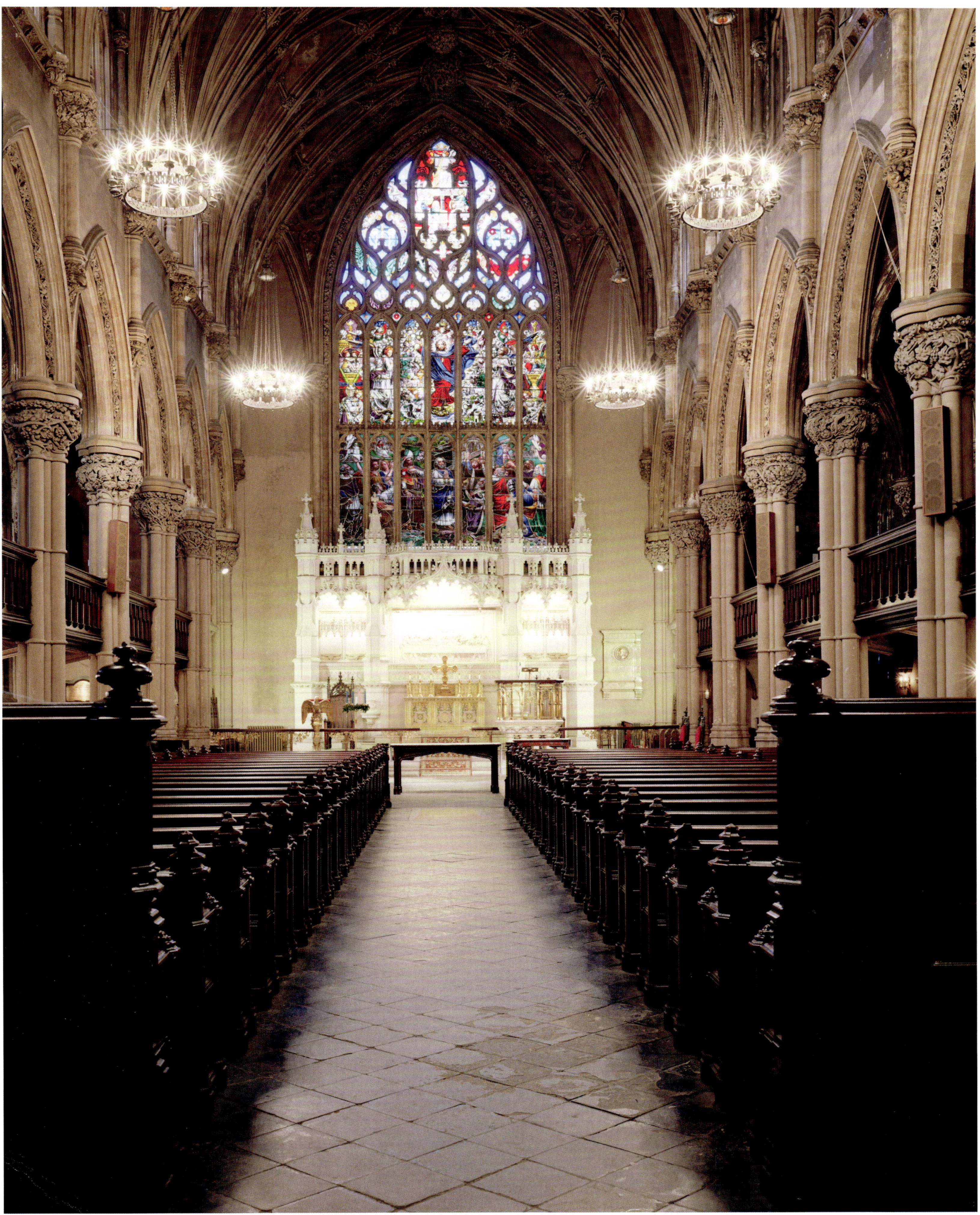

Nas couldn't make up his mind on how to rhyme
the first verse of "N.Y. State Of Mind" from his debut
album "Illmatic."
"I don't know how to start this shit," he said into
the microphone while speaking to his producer,
DJ Premier. Then, all of a sudden, he started rapping
a 60-bar verse that he had just written that day about
his rapping skills and the dangerous New York streets
where he grew up.
He recorded the song in just one take.

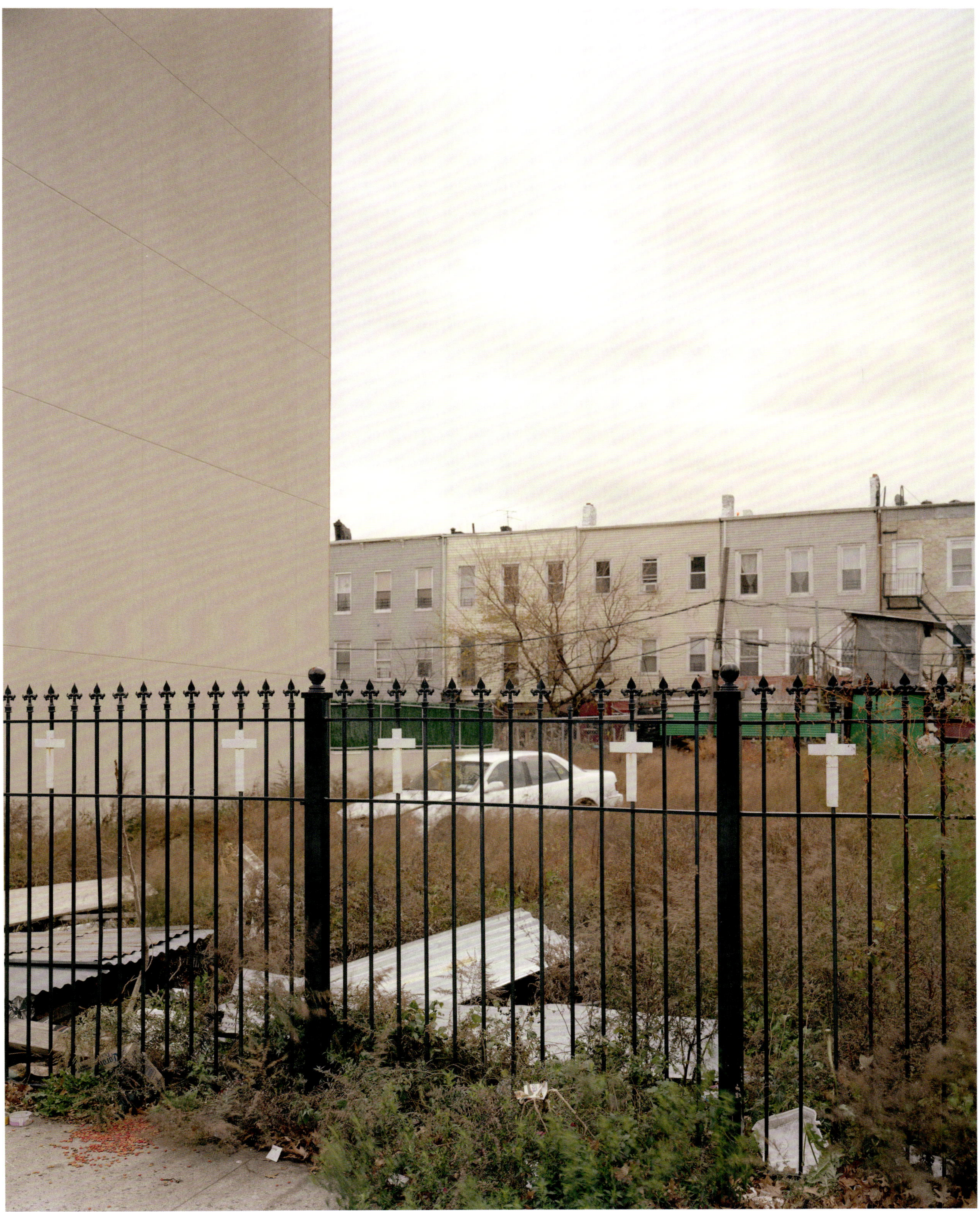

Jimi Hendrix had a girlfriend named Monique. She used
to spend a lot of time at 321 East 9th Street on the Lower East
Side in a dress shop that was owned by two friends of hers.
Jimi would sit in the shop and pretend to be the salesman,
blowing the minds of customers by coming out from behind
the curtain and telling them how good they looked.

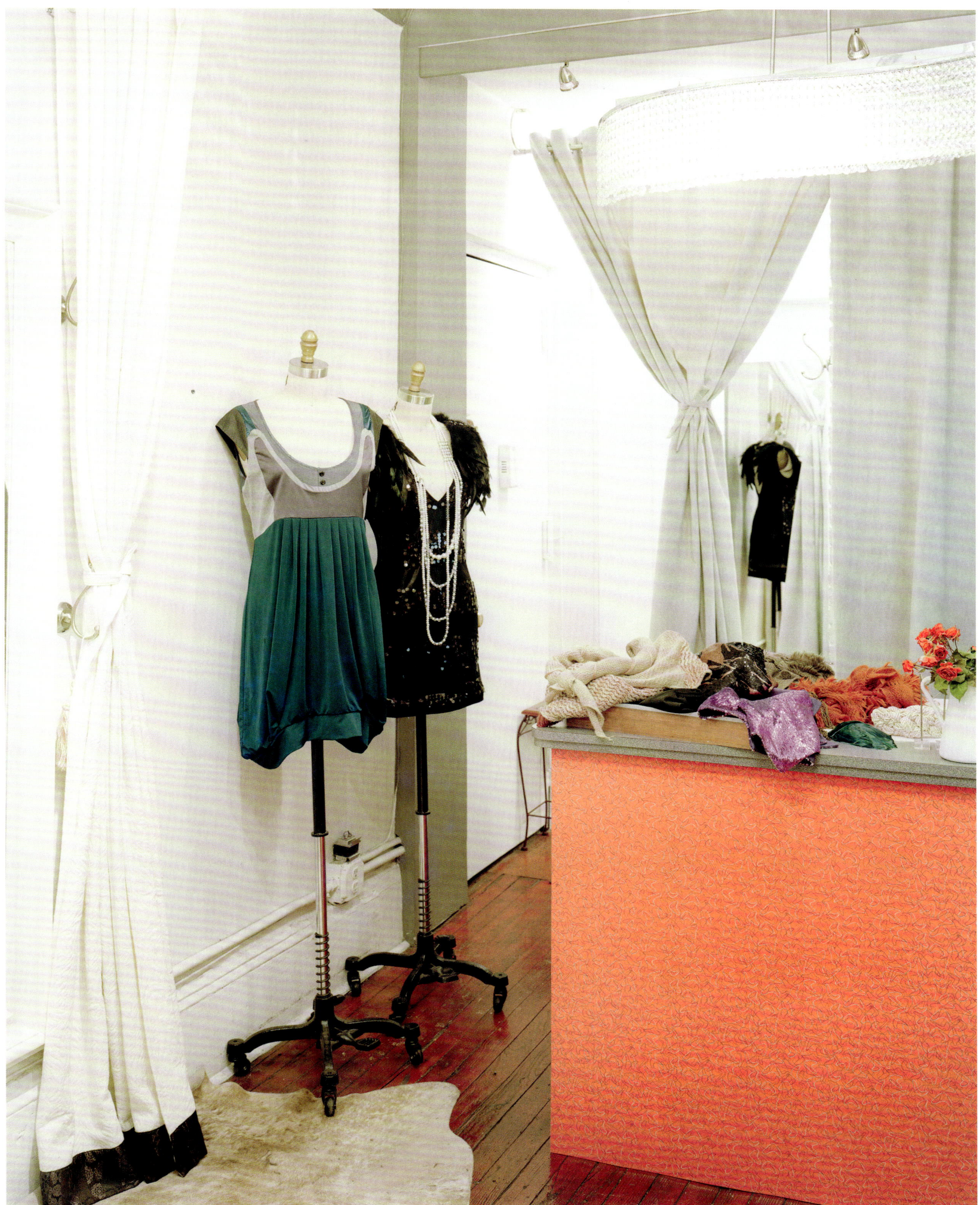

In 1974, William Burroughs arrived in New York.
Allen Ginsberg got him a contract to teach creative writing
at City College. He found an apartment at 222 Bowery,
affectionately nicknamed "The Bunker."
On February 28, 1974, *Rolling Stone* magazine published
an extensive interview between William Burroughs
and David Bowie, "Beat Godfather Meets Glitter Mainman."
Bowie was surprised and delighted when Burroughs
told him that the heroes of one of his latest novels, *The Wild Boys*,
carried an 18-inch "Bowie knife" as a weapon.

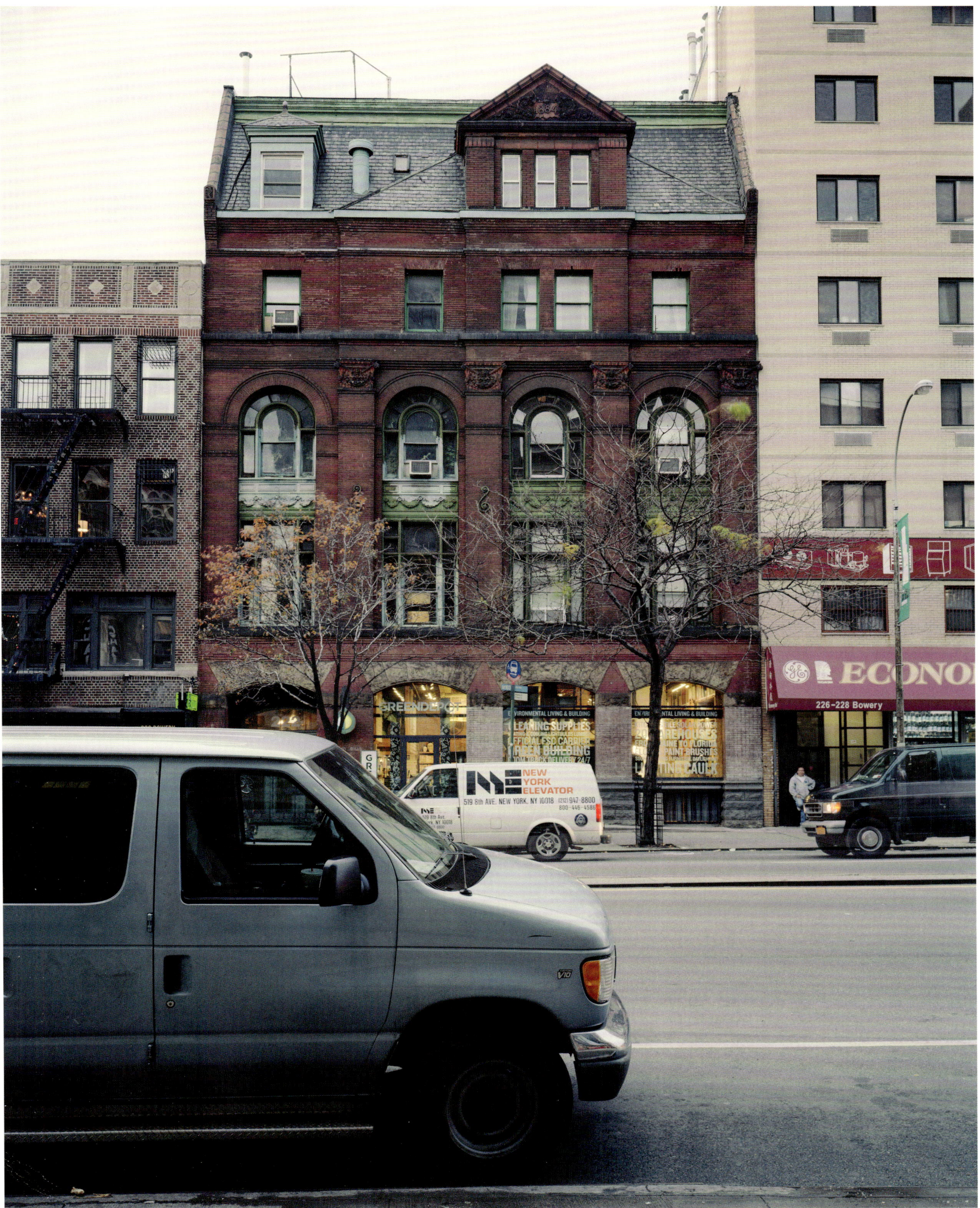
226-228 Bowery
ECONO
GREENDPO
ENVIRONMENTAL LIVING & BUILDING
LEARNING SUPPLIES
NEW
YORK
ELEVATOR
519 8th AVE. NEW YORK, NY 10018
(212) 947-8800
800-446-4586

Kiss played their very first concert on January 30, 1973
at Popcorn, a club on 4703 Queens Boulevard under
the shadow of the 7 viaduct.
There were less than ten people in attendance, including
the bar staff.

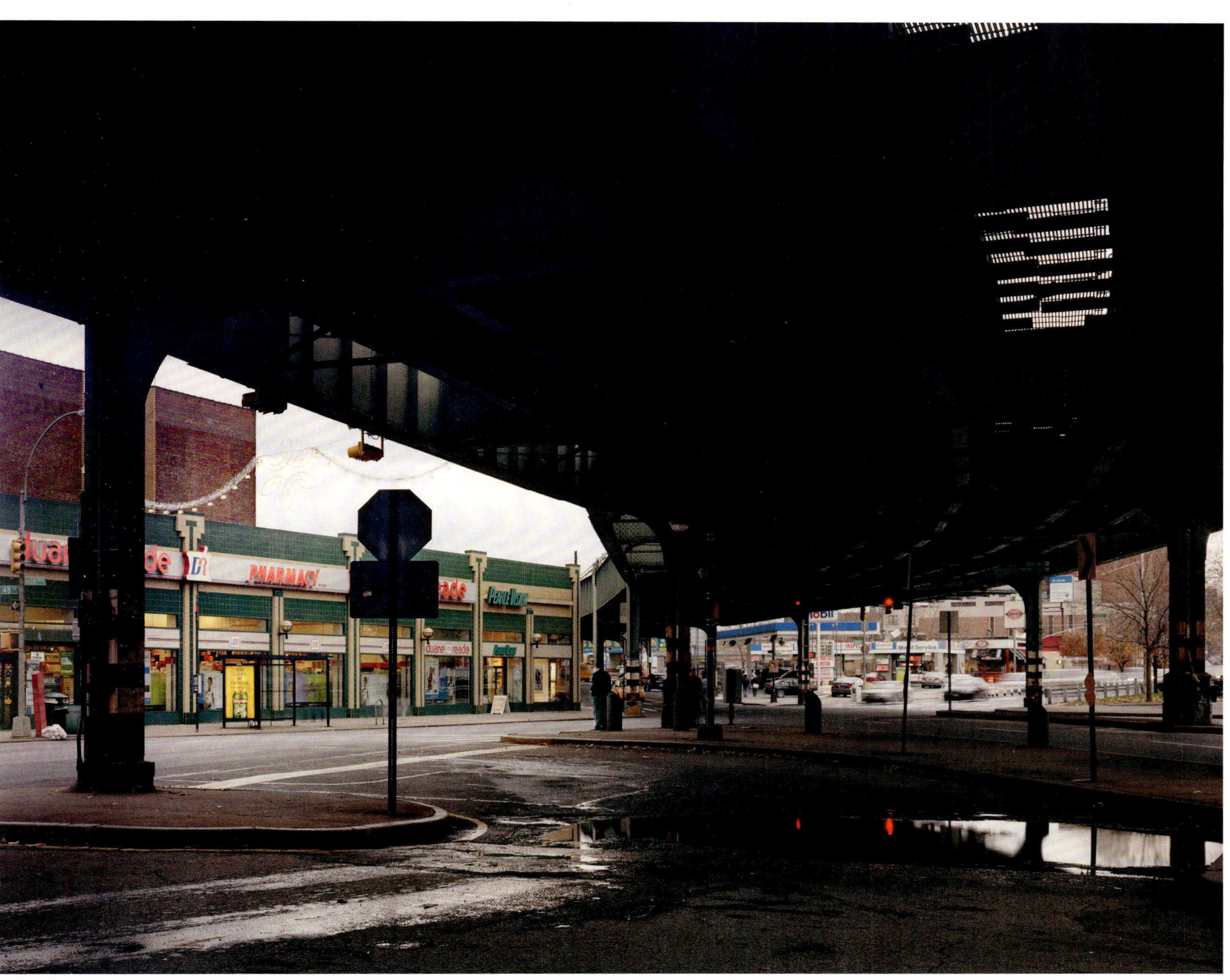

PHARMACY
Duane reade
PEARLE VISION
Duane reade
Mobil

Native New Yorker Dave Van Ronk was one of the leading
figures of the Greenwich Village acoustic folk scene
in the early 1960s.
He was leading coffehouse folk culture and inspiring many
upcoming artists, including Bob Dylan.
He was nicknamed the "Major of MacDougal Street."
His apartment at 15 Sheridan Square was a meeting place
for all the artists and musicians in Greenwich Village.
Bob Dylan spent many nights sleeping on his couch during
his first winter in New York.

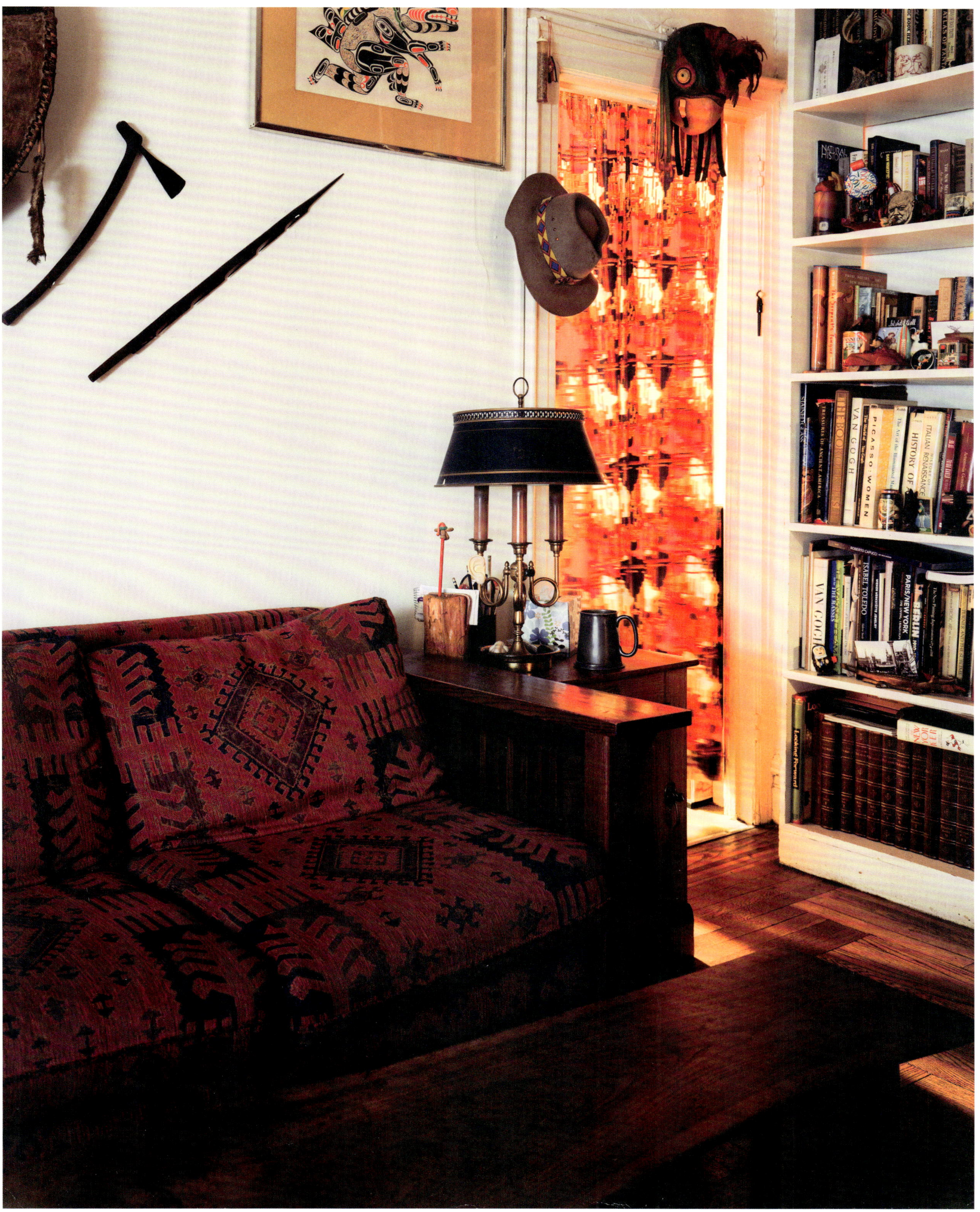

On April 2, 2011 LCD Soundsystem played what
they had announced as their last concert at Madison
Square Garden.
After nearly four hours of performing, James Murphy
took the front stage to play the last song of the set:
"New York I Love You But You're Bringing Me Down."

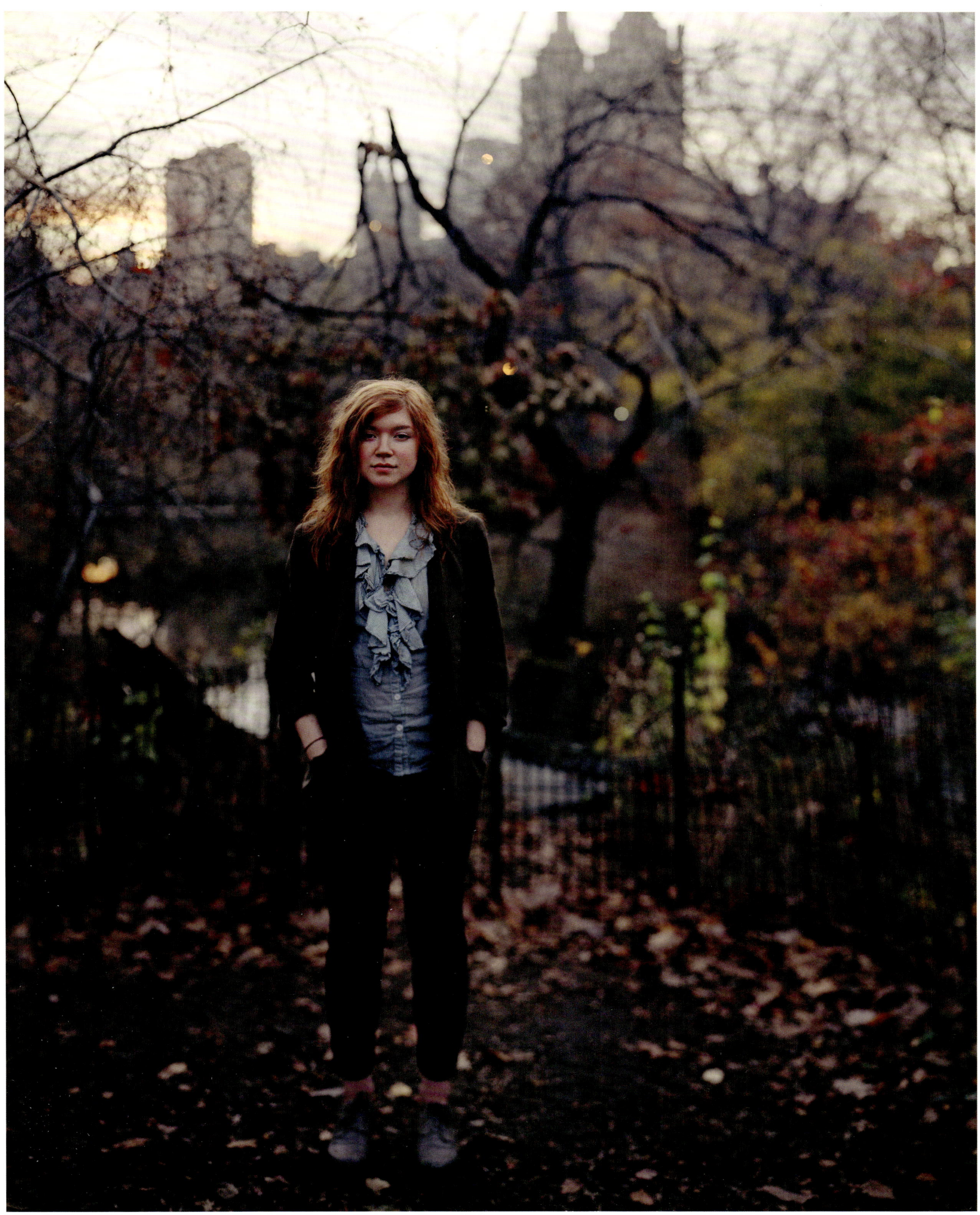

Suzanne Vega was sitting at a corner table waiting for
her cup of coffee when she wrote the song "Tom's Diner."
In the lyrics, she recalls reading in a newspaper a story about
the death of a famous actor who had an alcohol problem.
The New York Post featured a front-page story
on William Holden, star of *The Bridge On River Kwai*
who died alone and drunk in his Santa Monica home and
was found dead four days later.
It was November 18, 1981.

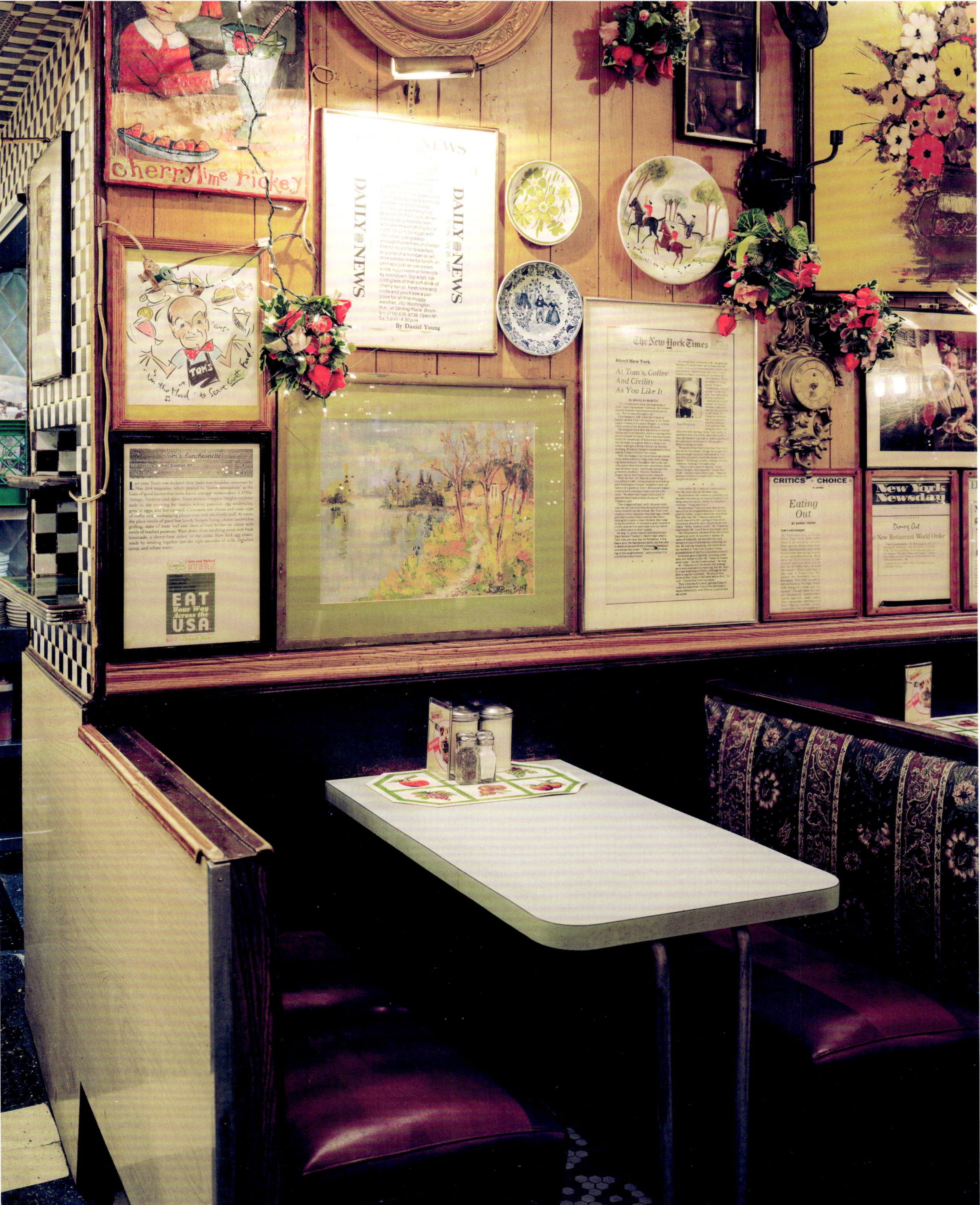
cherry lime rickey
DAILY NEWS
DAILY NEWS
By Daniel Young
The New York Times
About New York
At Tom's, Coffee
And Civility
As You Like It
Tom's Luncheonette
EAT
Your Way
Across the
U.S.A.
CRITICS' CHOICE
Eating
Out
BY DANIEL YOUNG
New York
Newsday
The New Restaurant World Order

On June 19, 2011, prog-rock band Oneida held a special
performance at the art venue Secret Project Robot in
Williamsburg to celebrate the release of their new album,
"Absolute II."
They played their previous two albums "Preteen Weaponry"
and "Rated O" along with "Absolute II" from dusk to dawn.
Secret Project Robot closed in the fall of 2011.

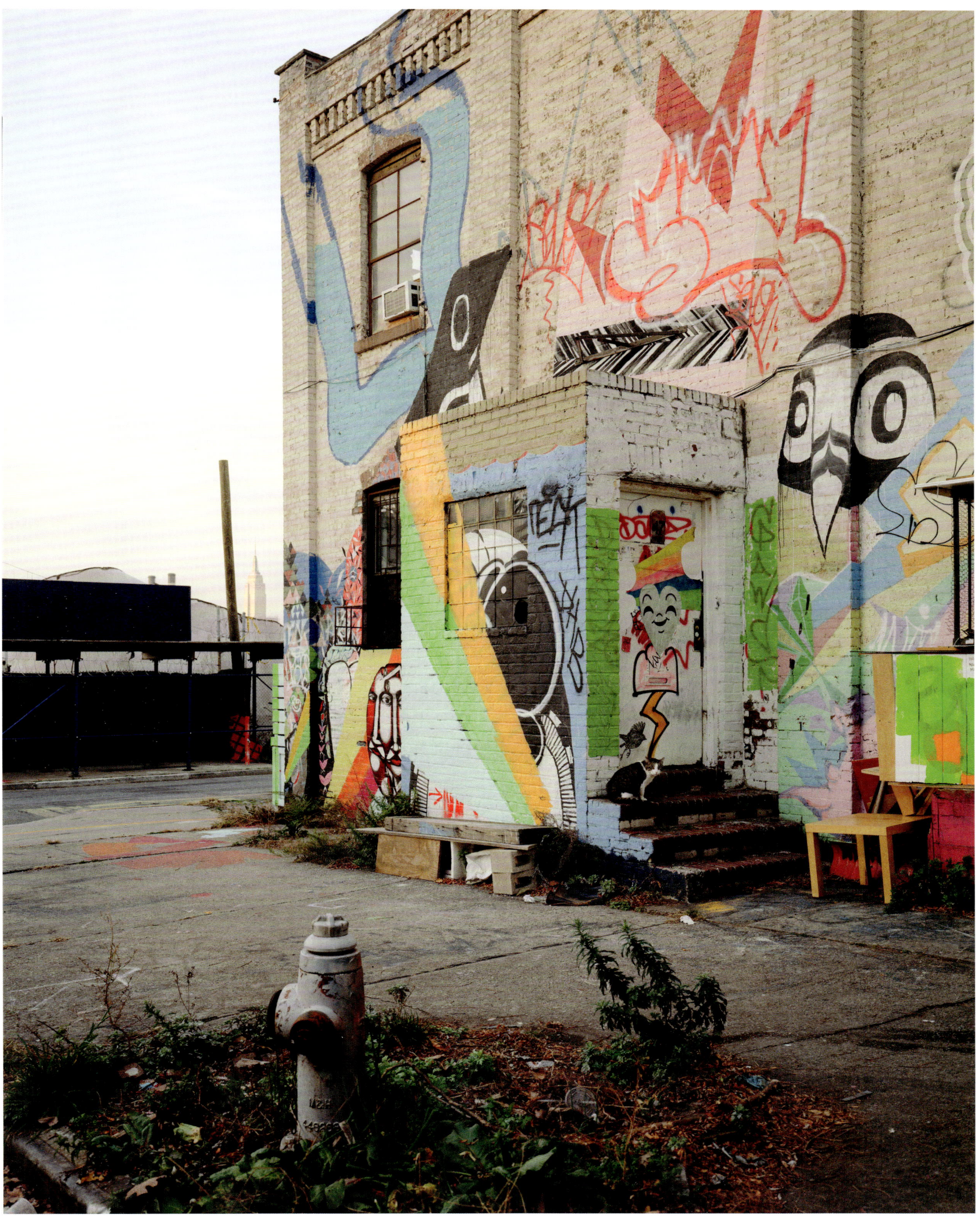

In July 1965, John Cale shared a fifth-floor apartment
at 56 Ludlow Street with experimental filmmaker
Tony Conrad for 25 dollars a month.
It was here that Lou Reed, Sterling Morrison, and John Cale
rehearsed and taped on a Wollensak recorder the very
first songs of their band, The Velvet Underground.

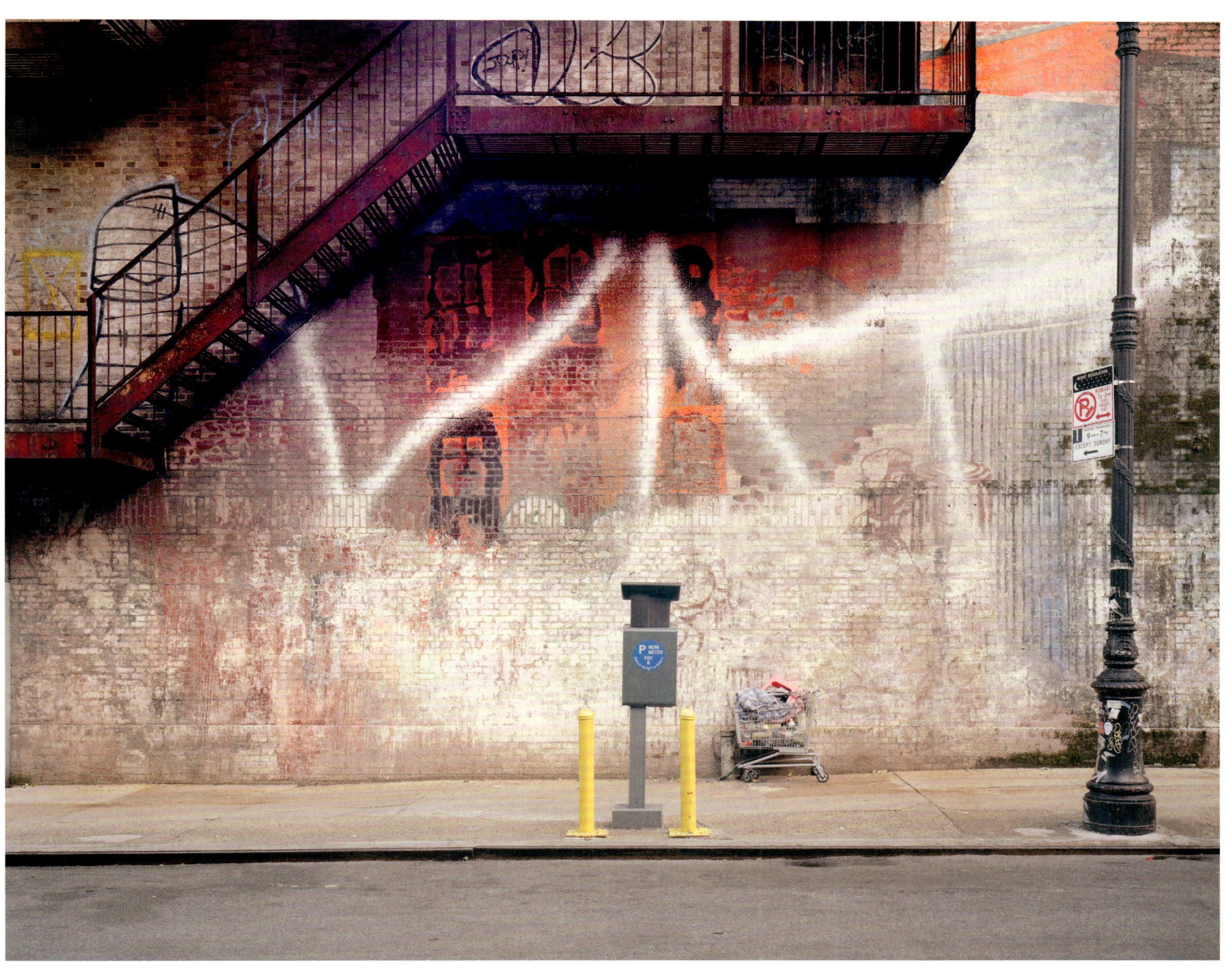

In 1969, Paul Simon wrote "The Only Living Boy In New York"
dedicated to his childhood friend Art Garfunkel,
who was going to Mexico to pursue his new acting career.
It was released on January 26, 1970 on the fifth
Simon & Garfunkel album, "Bridge Over Troubled Water,"
which topped the charts in ten countries and received
two Grammy Awards.
Paul Simon and Art Garfunkel split up soon after the album
was released. They had debuted in 1957 under the name
"Tom & Jerry" while they were still students at Forest Hills
High School in Queens.

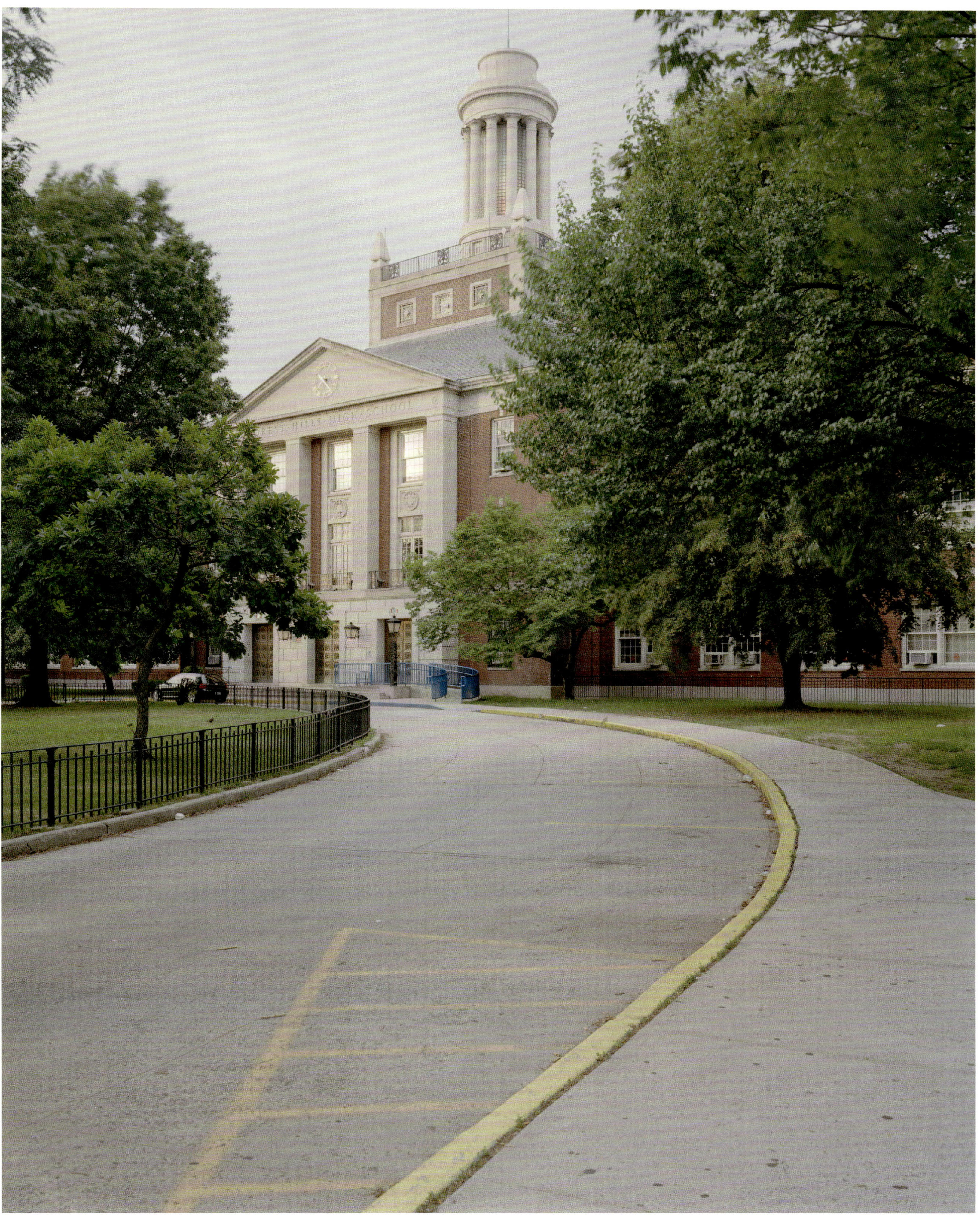

"I was looking for a place to stay on the Lower East Side
and I was desperate. The entire place was an open-air
drug supermarket.
One day, eventually, I found this place. It was real, so close
to the nude essence of the city. It became my art space.
My door was always open, and one day a young kid named
Douglas Colvin stepped in and said: 'Hi, I like the music
you're listening to.'
That kid was Dee Dee Ramone, and my place became
the headquarter of The Ramones."

Arturo Vega (October 13, 1947 – June 8, 2013)

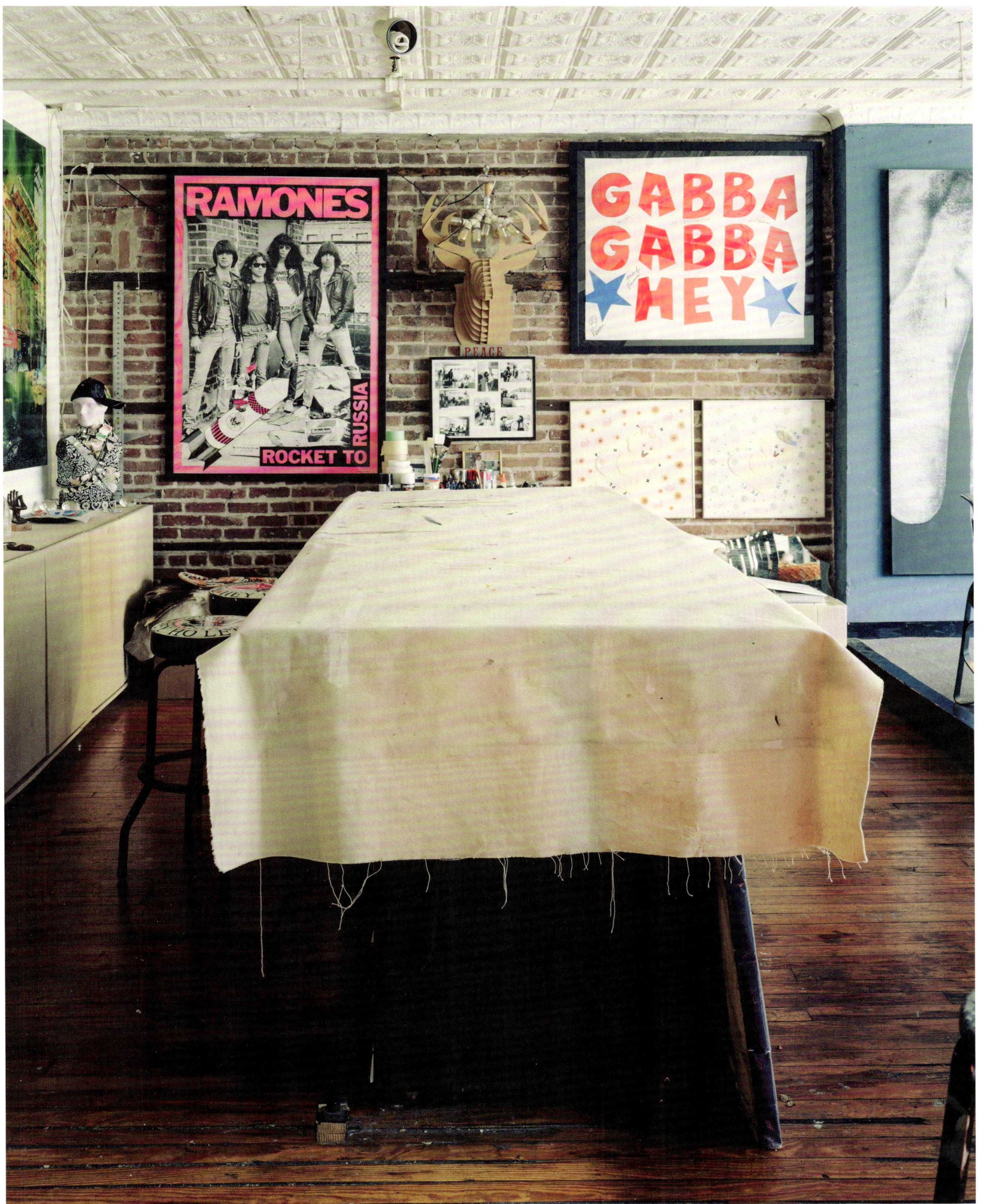

RAMONES
ROCKET TO RUSSIA
GABBA
GABBA
HEY
PEACE

New York Serenade is a thematic tour across places in New York City related to the history of rock music. Schiappa shows us how, within a globalized and homogenized urban space, one can still find local specificity and cultural authenticity by salvaging the stories and memories connected to certain locations. What makes the project particularly interesting is that far from activating regressive nostalgia towards a more "authentic" past, Schiappa places next to each other the undifferentiated and de-territorialized city on the one hand, and the uniqueness of places as real as material facts on the other. Rather than conflicting, these two different ways of conceiving the city co-exist within a time frame that is constantly poised between past and present, speed and slowness, highlighting the historical dimension of urban spaces. The photographer's retrieval of memories and atmospheres belonging to New York City's rock scene is partly operated by the use of texts that accompany the images as legends. Thoughts and recollections of pop stars and stories about the places in the pictures merge with the photographs to create an interplay through which we learn about the boutique where Jimi Hendrix spent most of his afternoons; the settlement house on the Lower East Side that, after having been transformed into a condominium in the 1980s, became the home of Iggy Pop; the tiny town house where Patti Smith and Robert Mapplethorpe lived together; the small commercial building on Norfolk Street that once hosted the Tonic Club; The Bottom Line's previous and final location now transformed into a New York University office; the Sin-é on St. Mark's Place where young Irish immigrants gathered in the late 1980s and where artists such as Sinéad O'Connor performed. By establishing a relationship with places based on intimacy and affection, Schiappa depicts our relationship with urban spaces as simultaneously made of adjacencies and distances between past and present, between places, persons, objects, thoughts, and words. This way, he offers an enriching contribution to the fields of social documentary and street photography.

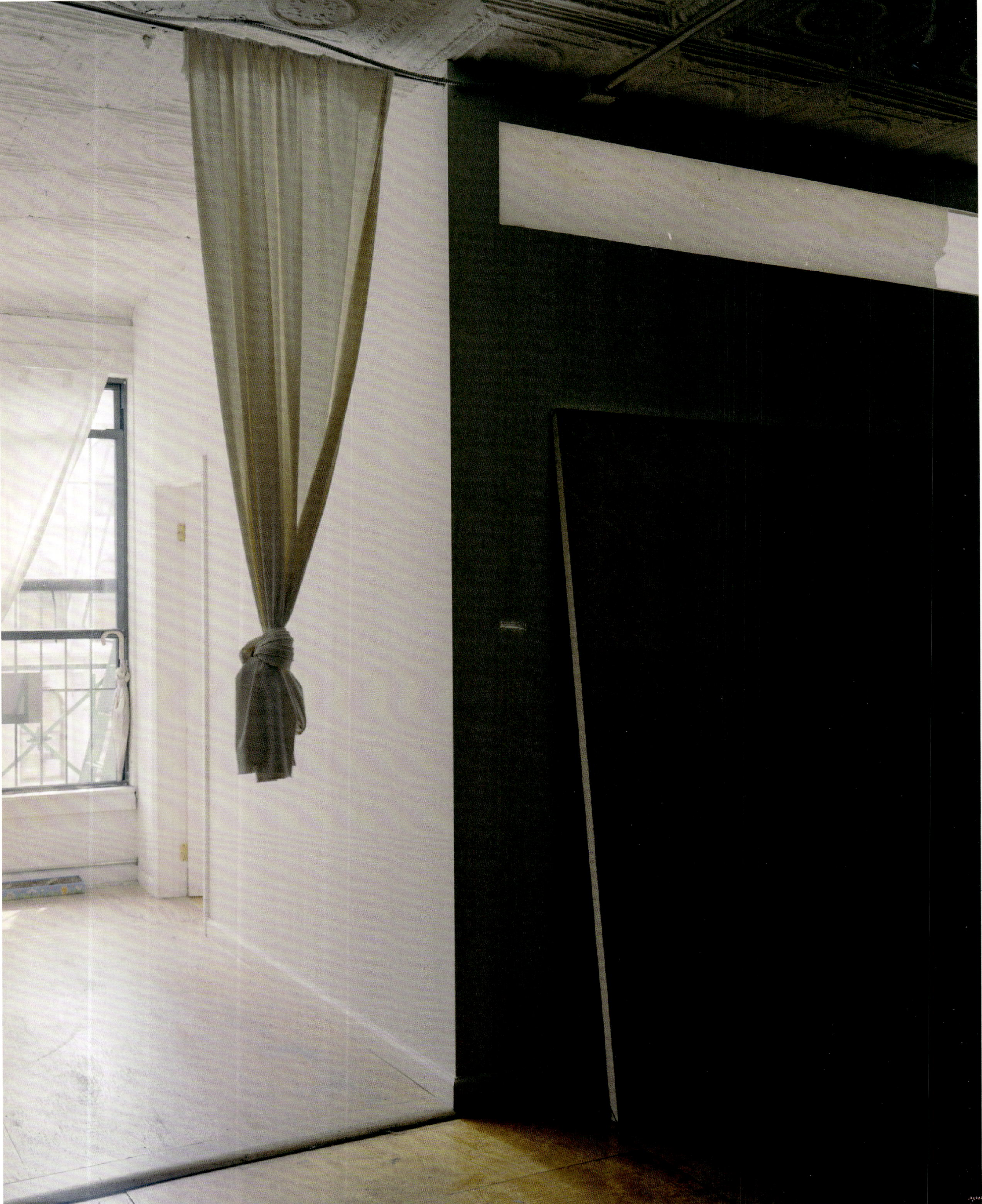

Thanks to

Joel Meyerowitz, Maggie Barrett, Nicoletta Leonardi, Gianfranco Mauti, Anna Marrucchi, Carlo Salvatori, Sergio Juan, Florencia Helguera, Irati García, Amalia Rusconi-Clerici, BLB studio legale, Alessandro Benedetti, Donato Silvano Lorusso, Piero Maranghi, Annie Marie McLaughlin, Ciro Schiappa, Maurizio Primi, Francesca Cremonesi, Carlo Cremonesi, Gretel Malmsheimer, Paola Mattei, Giuseppe Mauti, Luigi Mauti, Matteo Mauti, Louise Schiappa, Tomaso Piva, Eleonora Mocenni, Little Birds Gallery, Christine Ordioni, Rita Sberlati, Laurence Carles, Ember Rilleau, Gus Powell, John Saponara, Fiona Gilmour, Andy Friedman, Heather Bennett, Julian Swanson, Chad Lackow, Melanie Meijer, Tuttitrendy Boutique, Lenny Kaye, Ariel Agai, Jeanette Vuocolo, Irina Shabayeva, Rita Sà, Toni Toscano, Laura Toscano, Sandra Pires, Roland Vajs, Michele Palazzo, Lorenza Cerbin, Captain James "Rocky" Robinson and Bed-Stuy Volunteer Ambulance Corps, Stefano Colombo, Enrica Mosciaro, Mattia Insolera, Andrea Jurman, Paola Manzoni, Matteo Maresi, Tiziana Bonanni, Assunta Sarlo, Angelo Miotto, Max Menegazzi, Omar Schillaci, Roberto Brunelli, Annachiara Sacchi, Paola Maugeri, Sergio Praticò, Dani Aguilar, Alfredo Rodolfi, Valentina Dragoni, Dimitri Leboff, Antonia Raccat, Fondazione Studio Marangoni, Martino Marangoni, Alessandra Capodacqua, Arianna Rinaldo, Michele Lupi, Gabriele Basilico, Giovanna Calvenzi, Mario Govino, Mauro Telò, Raffaello Conti, Luca Fanfani, Valeria Corbetta, Roberto Battaglia, Pino Rozzi, Peppe Cirillo, Rosa Marzullo.

To Arturo Vega and Andrea Vuocolo for allowing us to shoot pictures inside their apartments.

And most of all to Maria Mauti for her emotional support and commitment.

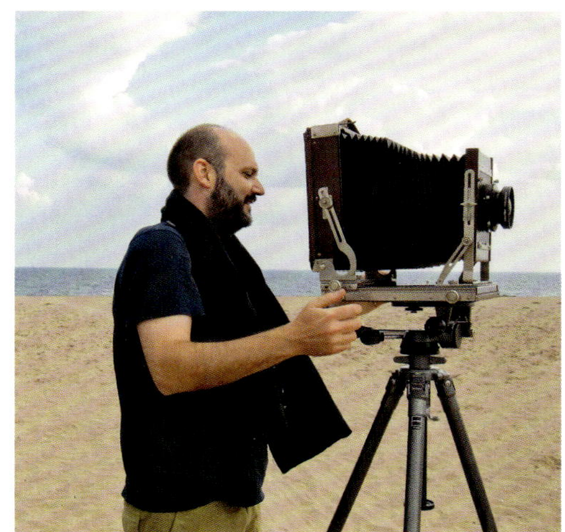 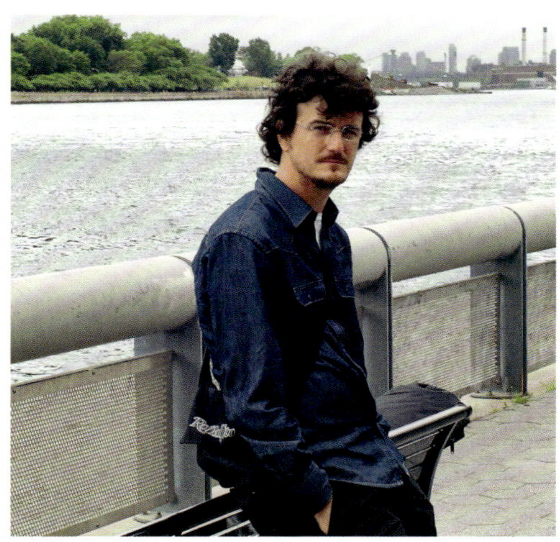

Ciro Frank Schiappa

Ciro Frank Schiappa was born in 1971
in Dublin, Ireland. He studied photography
at Fondazione Studio Marangoni in Florence,
Italy. His photographs have been featured
in numerous solo and group exhibitions,
including the 1997 European Young Artist
Biennal in Turin, the international
photography festival of Arles, the Art Institute
of Chicago, and the Galleria Civica
in Modena, his hometown.

Schiappa's twin photographic interests
in portraiture and architecture have continued
to develop in his subsequent series
beginning with his "Circostanze Familiari"
and continuing on to include "Leicamix"
and "Maremmana" in which he focuses on
how human nature relates to the environment.

Schiappa lives and works between
Barcelona and Milan.

www.cirofrankschiappa.com

Michele Primi

Michele Primi was born in Milan in 1973.
He has also lived in Barcelona and New York.

He is a journalist at *Rolling Stone* and writes
rock history programs for Virgin Radio.
He also contributes to *Wired*, *GQ*, *Icon*,
and *La Stampa*. He has worked for MTV
and has written music and rock culture
monographs. In 2008, he published the
volume *Queen* and in 2014 he published the
book *Tragedies and Mysteries of Rock 'n' Roll*.

Art Director
Sergio Juan

Design
Sergio Juan Design Office, Barcelona

Editorial Coordination
Vincenza Russo

Editing
Emily Ligniti

Layout
Irati Garcia for Sergio Juan Design Office

Translation
Gordon Fisher, Traduzioni Liquide

First published in Italy in 2016 by
Skira editore S.p.A.
Palazzo Casati Stampa
via Torino 61
20123 Milano
Italy
www.skira.net

Printed and bound in Italy.
First edition

ISBN: 978-88-572-3250-8

Distributed in USA, Canada, Central & South
America by Rizzoli International Publications, Inc.,
300 Park Avenue South, New York, NY 10010, USA.
Distributed elsewhere in the world by Thames
and Hudson Ltd., 181A High Holborn, London
WC1V 7QX, United Kingdom.